EBURY PRESS
FORGIVENESS IS A CHOICE

Kia Scherr has spent twenty years studying, practising and teaching at the Sanctuary Holistic Retreat Center in Virginia, United States. After her husband and thirteen-year-old daughter were killed in the Mumbai terror attack of 2008, Kia co-founded One Life Alliance (www.onelifealliance.org) to teach peace education programmes based on love, compassion and forgiveness. Kia spent six years in Mumbai, working with businesses, educationists and the police. *Forgiveness Is a Choice* is her debut book.

T0062016

Forgiveness Is a Choice

TEACHINGS ABOUT PEACE & LOVE

KIA SCHERR

EBURY
PRESS

An imprint of Penguin Random House

EBURY PRESS

USA | Canada | UK | Ireland | Australia
New Zealand | India | South Africa | China

Ebury Press is part of the Penguin Random House group of companies
whose addresses can be found at global.penguinrandomhouse.com

Published by Penguin Random House India Pvt. Ltd
4th Floor, Capital Tower 1, MG Road,
Gurugram 122 002, Haryana, India

Penguin
Random House
India

First published in Ebury Press by Penguin Random House India 2021

Copyright © Kia Scherr 2021

All rights reserved

10 9 8 7 6 5 4 3 2 1

The views and opinions expressed in this book are the author's own and the facts
are as reported by her which have been verified to the extent possible, and the
publishers are not in any way liable for the same.

ISBN 9780143450573

Typeset in Bembo Std by Manipal Technologies Limited, Manipal

This book is sold subject to the condition that it shall not, by way of trade
or otherwise, be lent, resold, hired out, or otherwise circulated without the
publisher's prior consent in any form of binding or cover other than that in
which it is published and without a similar condition including this condition
being imposed on the subsequent purchaser.

www.penguin.co.in

To Alan and Naomi

Contents

Introduction

My story of forgiveness

On Wednesday, 26 November 2008, as I was preparing a cup of tea at my mother's house in Florida, the phone rang. I casually picked it up and heard the frantic voice of my friend and colleague: 'Kia, turn on the news, the Oberoi hotel is being attacked by terrorists.' I dropped the phone and fell to the floor as I cried out to my mother to turn on the news. There it was—smoke pouring out of the iconic Taj hotel—but no mention of the Oberoi. That came later. As we hoped and prayed for the safety of Alan and Naomi, my husband and thirteen-year-old daughter, two days passed before the fateful phone call from the US consulate in Mumbai. 'I'm so sorry, Mrs Scherr. Both your husband and daughter were shot and killed in the restaurant at the Oberoi hotel. Their bodies have now been identified.'

Life as I knew it ended in that moment. For Alan and Naomi, their trip to India was meant to be the journey of a lifetime—a dream come true for Naomi, who was thrilled to visit the beautiful, exotic, colourful and amazing Mumbai, known as the city of dreams.

As their bodies lay lifeless under a table in the luxurious Oberoi hotel, I was in a strange twilight zone somewhere in the middle of a quiet gated senior community in sunny Florida with palm trees swaying in a gentle breeze outside. Inside the house, the news announcer brought me back to the devastating reality that Alan and Naomi were two of the murdered victims of a terrorist attack.

Numb with shock and disbelief, my family and I sat in the living room and watched the aftermath of the attack to find out more information. There he was, Ajmal Kasab—the lone surviving terrorist. Each of his nine colleagues had been killed, but he had survived, having been captured in a heroic effort by Mumbai police. In that moment, I heard the words of Jesus Christ float through my thoughts: 'Forgive them; they know not what they do.'

I said aloud to my family, 'We must forgive them. There is already too much hate. We must send love and compassion.' A ray of peace entered my heart, and I knew that was what I had to do in order to survive this. In those first few hours after I received the news, every breath was an effort.

'There is a crack in everything. That's how the light gets in.'—Leonard Cohen, Canadian folksinger

It took many years for me to truly experience that forgiveness is the light that gets in through the cracks, seeping in through the pieces of my shattered heart. The moment

I said yes to that inner voice was the moment I began to heal. I can't say I knew what it was to truly forgive, but I knew I didn't want to be held hostage by hatred and anger for the rest of my life. I refused to become a victim. I was still alive, and I could bring forth the opposite of hate. I could learn to love like an extremist. What would that mean? How would I go about it?

'How could you forgive a terrorist?' I was asked. Good question. Terrorism is a brutal attack against humanity. Unforgiveable. But on the other hand . . .

'We all come from the same Source. We are one human family.'—Saadi Shirazi, Persian poet

If this is true, and to me it feels like it is, then a person who could become a terrorist has forgotten this connection. He has forgotten who he is as a human being. To this extent, he is capable of killing innocent people. If I live in resentment and hatred for his disregard for human life, for his disconnection from the source of who he really is, then it is I who am held hostage by terrorism. I would be joining the terrorist in hatred. Is this how I want to live? No. Is this how I want to honour the lives of my husband and daughter, who were killed by a young man who forgot who he was? No, I feel compassion for a person who forgot who he was and lost his connection to love. I have not forgotten my connection to love, and therefore I want to live in love and harmony with my fellow human beings. I want to live in peace. I want to learn about the diversity of this magnificent fabric of life, to honour that diversity and celebrate our differences. This is a personal choice. It does not mean that the perpetrators should not be punished to the full extent of the law. Actions have consequences.

I am responsible for my actions, and I want to live my life in the most loving way that I can. Those that break the law need to be held accountable. Forgiveness does not mean letting them off the hook. Forgiveness takes the hook of hatred out of *our* hearts. That hook hurts no one but ourselves. Once you understand this, forgiveness is the obvious choice. You may not get there right away. It may take years. I wrote this book to help you get there. These practices will open your heart and you will find love waiting with open arms to embrace you.

This is a book about the choices I made to resurrect my life day by day, step by step. I asked myself, 'How can I honour life today?' 'How can I love?' The choices are simple, maybe even obvious, and yet putting them into practice is a journey of a lifetime. These choices represent various ways to be loving in practical life. It may be as simple as a smile you give to a clerk in a shop or practising patience with a small child. It may be listening with your full attention to a friend in need of comfort. Possibilities to express love are endless, but I will get you started with the ways I used to heal my life.

When I said yes to forgiveness, I said yes to love and saying yes to love was saying yes to the happenings of life that show up each day. When my husband and daughter were killed so dramatically, my life dissolved on so many levels. I found that the best way for me to live was to make a conscious intention to renew my life one day at a time. This was challenging at times, and sometimes felt impossible. Some days I did nothing at all but cry, pray and meditate. At some point in the midst of the tears, love came forward as a warm feeling in my heart. As I learnt to relax into this warmth, the sadness transmuted into love.

To increase love in everyday life, I had to bring my full attention to it. 'Whatever you put your attention on grows stronger in your life' is a teaching I have always remembered from Maharishi Mahesh Yogi. This is a profound practice that delivers results. What is it that you want to grow stronger in your life? What do you think about throughout your day? Notice your thoughts and use the power of intention to direct your attention to the best experiences possible—love, happiness, success, abundance, good health and peace—it's up to you.

Love shows up in many forms and is expressed in many different ways. This book outlines the ways I found to be the most helpful to generate love, compassion, peace and harmony in my life. Forgiveness is the key ingredient, the first step that unlocked the doors of my heart. To reach true forgiveness, I learnt how to open up in new ways, and this impacted how I related to each person in my life.

The purpose of this book is to make it easier for you to make these choices so that you can experience positive outcomes in every aspect of your life. We cannot control the happenings in our lives, but we can choose our responses. These choices can bring us closer to love or can take us further away from love. Every day presents opportunities to either increase or decrease love.

The experience of love enriches our lives. It connects us to people and builds harmonious relationships. When we love, we experience love. When we don't love, our hearts contract. When our hearts contract we shrink ourselves as we pull back from life. The more we pull back, the less happiness, fulfilment and love we will experience.

Why is forgiveness a choice?

Self-mastery is the recognition that you have a choice as to how you respond to your life situations and then making choices that empower you and your life. This is not a self-help book. My intention is to show you how to master your life through the power of choice and to provide examples of the choices you can make each day to empower your life. There are choices that lead to forgiveness, where forgiveness is a natural outcome of self-love. By the time you get to the point of forgiveness, it's almost a choiceless choice—it's not something you do, it's simply an outcome that opens your heart to a deeper experience of life. Forgiveness will bring you peace. Forgiveness will transform you from the inside out. Forgiveness will strengthen your heart, making it more resilient and flexible to manage life's challenges effectively.

I invite you to join me on this path of forgiveness. Step by step, day by day, love will grow stronger, and before long, love will become your most natural way of being. May you be blessed with an abundance of love, joy, compassion and peace.

How to use this book

This book outlines thirty practices that I used to renew my life after a major loss that turned everything I knew upside down. Forgiveness was the key that kept my heart open to love, but we don't begin with forgiveness.

We want to lead up to forgiveness after we have reached some understanding and acceptance of what has happened. The ultimate outcome is increasing your experience of love, so it's worth taking this step by step, day by day.

We make choices every day. What we choose determines the outcome of our experiences each day. I learnt that when I took the time to reflect and make intentional choices based on creating positive outcomes, I could enjoy the flow of life in a new way. I learnt to live with love and bring joy back into my life.

To gain the full benefit of these simple practices, it is best to focus on one practice at a time, day by day or even longer. You may read through the whole book or just read one chapter a day. Writing down the day's focus on a calendar or in a journal is a tremendous help—I still write intentions daily and am often surprised by how many blessings manifest as a result.

1

Slow Down

'Slow down and everything you are chasing will come around and catch you.'—John De Paola

When life took an unexpected turn, I found myself moving in slow motion. Nothing about my life would ever be the same. Slowing down became a gift, and I realized the value of not pushing to get things done. Almost everything can wait. We miss so much detail when we rush through our day. To intentionally slow down is a powerful choice. It is the first step to masterful living. There are many situations we cannot control. We cannot turn back time to change an event, but we can create the most positive outcomes when we take the time to be fully present. We need to pay attention. After the Mumbai terrorist attack, I had a lot of time for reflection. I knew who I was in relation to my roles as wife and mother. I am still a mother, but my sons are now grown and no longer live with me. Who am I now? I had to slow down and find out.

What will you learn about yourself when you slow down? This is worth exploring.

How to begin? Just stop for a moment and be still. Look around you wherever you are. What do you see? What do you hear? What do you smell? What time of day is it?

Before you rush off to start your activity of the day, just be still for a moment or two.

What thoughts arise? How do you feel? What needs to get done today? What do you want to do today? What is required of you to do your best, be your best and succeed in your responsibilities?

You have a whole day before you waiting to come to life with you in it. How will you be? Just being alive in this moment is worth a smile. Take a long, deep breath and allow yourself to relax. Relax for a moment and let your thoughts settle down as you breathe slowly. A relaxed mind will bring clarity of thinking and creative inspiration.

I enjoy slowing down in busy places like Mumbai. There is so much bustling, and everyone is moving fast. Cars are crawling along at a slow pace because of all the traffic. In Mumbai I especially like sitting in a black and yellow cab with all the noisy honking and crowds of people packing every open space on the pavement. I love the contrast of the busy crowds and the slow traffic. I saw a lot of big, beautiful smiles, children playing games, people selling flowers, chai, delicious food and colourful scarves. The city was moving fast, but I was slowed down and was able to watch and enjoy one of the most vibrant cultures in the world.

When I took the time to slow down every day, I learnt to speak less and listen more. Slowing down allows for experiences such as joy to flow into our lives. Joy bubbles up from within when we take the time to notice it. Otherwise, there is no time for joy if we stomp over it in our rush to get on with our day. Slowing down will bring forth surprising experiences that are missed when you are moving too fast to notice.

Here are the statements of intention I used to remind myself to slow down. To speak or write out your intention will empower the experience you choose to have. Repeat these statements aloud or silently to yourself with long slow breaths. Pause for a few seconds between each statement in order for it to settle into your awareness.

- Today, I am willing to relax and let go.
- I am enjoying a slower pace in my thoughts, words and actions.
- I allow everything to unfold perfectly in its own time.
- As I slow down, I open myself to a more fulfilling experience of life.
- I am grateful for the life I am living as I slow down to fully experience this moment.

At the end of the day, it is helpful to take some time to reflect upon how slowing down made a difference in your experience today.

How often were you able to slow down and take your time without rushing?

Were you able to make some quiet time for yourself for at least ten to fifteen minutes? What insights did you gain?

What did you notice about your surroundings when you slowed down?

What did you notice about your interactions with friends and family when you slowed down?

Did anything catch your attention that you would have missed if you did not slow down?

2

The Power of a Smile

'Sometimes your joy is the source of your smile, but sometimes your smile can be the source of your joy.'—*Thich Nhat Hanh*

I have learnt never to underestimate the power of a smile. Smiling is a sharing of positive energy—a simple sharing of your goodwill towards others and receiving their goodwill towards you. The sharing of smiles can take place even in the saddest of times. After my husband and daughter were killed, I thought I would never smile again, but so much love poured forth from around the world in the aftermath of the terrorist attack that I found myself smiling with appreciation for the compassion and loving support shared with me from people all over the world. I smiled in acknowledgement of the connection we all share as a world family. We don't always feel this connection— sometimes quite the opposite—but it is there underneath the surface.

It is easy to take smiles for granted. Sometimes we smile out of habit without any real feeling behind it. We have all seen fake smiles—the mouth may be shaped like a smile, but the eyes tell the truth—it is not a real smile if there is no light in the eyes. When I do encounter that light in the eyes along with the smiling mouth, it lights up my day.

When you slow down, you may find yourself smiling more often, sometimes for no reason other than to be alive. Isn't just being alive reason enough to smile? You won't notice being alive if you are caught up in the rush and noise of life.

Smiles are contagious. This works both ways. A few years ago, I was on my own in New York City, attending a three-day workshop with a group of people dedicated to creating projects for positive change. As I walked down Broadway in Manhattan, feeling somewhat nervous on the first day, I passed a man sweeping the pavement. Our eyes met, and he gave me a huge smile. I relaxed and smiled back. As I continued along, I smiled and kept on smiling as people returned my smile. This opened up a new attitude in me for New York.

I didn't expect New York to be such a friendly city. When I mentioned this to a fellow workshop participant, she told me that ever since 9/11, people in New York had become friendlier. Not what you would expect after a terrorist attack that killed 2000 people. Surviving tragedy gives us a renewed appreciation for life. Smiles connect strangers in a brief moment, a moment that acknowledges our shared existence. I learnt that day never to doubt the power of a smile.

One of the first things I noticed when I arrived in India was the abundance of smiles. People were smiling everywhere I looked. When eyes met, there was always a warm, welcoming smile. When I did a workshop with some students in South Mumbai, we discussed the experiences of slowing down, smiling and breathing deeply. When asked about what they had learnt with this practice, one of the girls said, 'I learnt I am prettier when I smile.' That is so true for each of us—our smiles help to create a more beautiful world.

One of the most beautiful smiles and one that is most contagious is a baby's smile. Parents are so excited by their baby's first smile that they tell all their friends about it when it happens. When each of my children smiled for the first time, I remember making calls to my husband and parents—'Aaron smiled!' 'Adam smiled!' 'Naomi smiled!' How amazing that such a simple smile can bring so much joy. Smiles bring joy and share joy. Joy is not something we can conjure up or manipulate; it just happens. Joy is a gift from life when it bubbles up in our hearts. Joy surprises us at times when we least expect it. When it happens for me, I feel so grateful and often get tears in my eyes. I have always loved these lines from a poem by William Blake:

> He who binds to himself a joy
> Does the winged life destroy;
> But he who kisses the joy as it flies
> Lives in eternity's sun rise.

Reading this short poem brings a smile to my face. We all know and love people who 'make us smile'. Smiles are such a joy to give and to receive, a fleeting joy that lights up our life in that moment.

If you wish to bring more beauty into this world with your smiles, not only does it feel good, it also forges a closer connection to others and creates a sense of well-being and happiness. I have found this to be a worthwhile practice on many occasions, especially when I am feeling sad.

First, set your intention to direct your smile focus for this day.

- Today, I will make it a point to smile as much as possible.
- I am smiling with understanding, love and compassion.
- Smiling opens my heart to the experience of joy.
- I am so grateful for the smile I experience in this moment.
- I will carry this focus with me throughout the day with love and gratitude.

To begin your day, look in the mirror and smile at yourself. It may feel forced at first, but you will soon smile and maybe even laugh when you try it.

Smile at the first person you see as you move about your day. Continue to greet each person with a smile from your eyes and heart as well as your face.

In addition to increasing your own smiles, notice the smiles around you. The more smiles you see, the more you will find yourself smiling. In the process of smiling, it is helpful to include a little smile for yourself. Smile at your humanness and your willingness to bring some cheer to your day. Smile with compassion and know you are doing the best you can. Let go and allow yourself to be as you are for this moment.

I find it helpful to reflect on my experience at the end of the day—both challenges and highlights. There is always a mix of events that flowed smoothly and events that did not work out so well. In this way I learn how I can make better choices or adjust my actions to create a positive outcome.

At the end of the day, what did you learn about yourself as a result of all the smiling? What did you learn about others?

What kinds of smiles did you notice?

Did you notice a light in the person's eyes when they smiled?

On this day may your life be lit up with smiles and may joy fill your hearts.

3

Breath, a Doorway into Peace

'Sometimes the most important thing in a whole day is the rest we take between two deep breaths.'—Etty Hillesum

Before we introduce the practices that lead to forgiveness, we need to slow down and learn to relax. It may feel challenging at first, but just by bringing your attention to your breath, you will quiet your mind. Better yet is to bring your breath to your heart. This is a magical place. Slowly and easily, breath by breath, you will soon settle into a state of peace. By using your attention, you can direct your focus to your breath. Breathing happens inside your body so this focus directs you inward without any effort. Attention to your breath brings you to the present moment. After a few breaths you may notice you're back to your thoughts. That's fine, just return to your breath over and over and you will settle down into a relaxed state.

Practise restful breathing

The best way to follow these instructions is to read one entry, pause to do as directed, then read the next.

- Find a quiet place to sit or stand still and simply allow yourself to feel. Notice your breath and breathe in slowly and deeply, then out slowly.
- Close your eyes. Notice the in and out rhythm of your breath. Let go of every concern and just be still.
- Remain unattached to your thoughts as they come and go. Just let them float through. Keep breathing and relaxing more with each breath.
- If you feel upset for any reason, impatient or bored or fidgety, just be with those feelings. Feel as much as you can and notice how much dissolves with each breath.
- Notice how becoming aware of your breathing slows you down. And, once you are slowed down, notice that you are experiencing more peace underneath the noise of your thoughts and feelings.

Understanding the practice

Breathing connects us to all of life. We breathe with awareness and remember that there is no life without breath. It is natural to feel grateful for this gift of life, coming to us in every breath, a gift that we share as we breathe out in return. We realize that we are breathing with gratitude.

Any sense of loneliness that we may carry begins to dissolve. We are not separate from life. As our awareness expands, our sense of self expands. 'I am more than this separate, little human. I am one with all of life, breathing with all living beings.'

Breathing this way keeps the energy inside you flowing with the dance of life, rather than clogging up with the stress of personal details. We begin to experience the mind as a vast ocean where thoughts are like waves on the surface and beneath the waves there is stillness, silence, peace.

Using this practice in your life

All of us have moments each day when we are between activities. We may be on the phone, waiting for an agent, listening to recorded music. We might be sitting at a traffic light, waiting for the signal to change. We might be waiting for software to load or for a waiter to bring our order. What do we do during these in-between moments?

Waiting can be boring or it can be interesting and even entertaining if we are observant. We often choose to direct our attention to a screen of some kind, usually our smartphone. We check for texts, for emails, we scan newsfeeds or surf through our Facebook or Instagram traffic.

It's possible to develop a different habit. You can use some of these moments, not for further engagement with a mental world 'out there' somewhere, but to connect with the very real and immediate inner world that reveals itself through conscious breathing. Learn to become fully present, for two seconds, for twenty, and begin to experience slowing down. Time does seem to slow, awareness expands, and the experience of life itself somehow becomes richer.

For me, when I close my eyes and dive beneath the waves, beneath thoughts and beneath feelings, I discover a deep inner silence, and in this silence, I find peace. The easiest way to dive in is through your breathing; close your eyes as you finish reading this sentence for a brief experience of stillness. Once you notice the stillness, you can return to it again and again. There is always stillness underneath the thoughts and the noise of life. I once tried this in a noisy cab in Mumbai, and even with all the honking, I experienced stillness simultaneous to the noise.

It's fun to experiment with this and makes for a much less aggravating cab ride.

Attention is a powerful tool because it is up to us where we choose to put our attention. Where we put our attention determines our experience. Breath is the first doorway to peace. It is the most accessible and easiest to focus upon. We are constantly breathing but hardly ever notice. When I adopted the practice of noticing my breath, I felt more alive and at peace with myself and the world.

4

Acceptance

'Accept your humanness as well as your divinity, totally and without reserve.'—Bernard Avishai

To accept our humanness we must be able to accept ourselves as we are. This doesn't mean we don't try to be our best and change what doesn't work. There are all kinds of changes we can make in our lives once we know what we want and what is required of us. To know what we want we must know who we truly are. I have found this to be a lifelong process with many twists and turns, some of which surprised and delighted me and some of which disappointed me. I'm learning to nurture the good parts and let go of or strengthen the weaknesses. But first, I must accept the imperfections. This is not a pleasant process and can even be painful at times, but when I have opened myself to all of who I am, it frees me to let go of what doesn't serve me so I can embrace what truly nurtures my spirit.

Acceptance is a willingness to meet ourselves and others without resistance or judgement. Resistance and judgement push life away from us, separating us from love and shutting down our hearts. Acceptance opens the heart and allows the flow of love. And a loving heart brings peace. It's a common misunderstanding that acceptance means forcing yourself to like a situation or someone's behaviour even if it doesn't appeal to you. It actually means accepting something for what it is, which then allows you to deal more effectively with the person or situation. We cannot control life, but we can direct our responses to the happenings of life. Accepting life as it shows up in our experience is meeting reality where it is in the present moment. Acceptance is the first step towards making a conscious choice that will result in a peaceful outcome for *ourselves*. But remember, it may take time.

The first step to acceptance is to slow down and breathe deeply. This will allow you to be open to accepting that which you may find unacceptable.

Each day presents numerous opportunities to practise acceptance. Some experiences require different degrees of acceptance. For example, the loss of a loved one is the most challenging experience to accept, but the more we resist, the more we will suffer. Suffering is always an option, but when suffering is turned into acceptance, peace prevails. With a peaceful heart and mind, we can determine what needs to be done. Or perhaps, no actions are necessary or even possible.

When something happens that feels unacceptable, it is natural to feel frustrated, angry, disappointed, hurt, sad or heartbroken. First and foremost, these feelings must be experienced fully and accepted because this is what you are experiencing in the immediate moment. This is the time to slow down and give yourself to completely feeling what is coming up, without resistance or judgement. This is a time to bring compassionate attention to yourself.

Acceptance of self

Most of us are acutely aware of our imperfections. At any point in our lives, we always have some complaint, 'my nose is too big', 'I could lose some weight around my stomach', 'I wish I earned more money', 'I'm not patient enough', 'I don't have the talent to play an instrument' are the types of things we tell ourselves and others. While it is always possible to do better and to be better, the first step is to accept ourselves as we are.

When I compare myself to other people, I feel lacking in some way. I feel as if I am not good enough. I may feel you are good at some things, but not at others. But isn't that the same for everyone? We each have different flaws and imperfections. We each have gifts and talents that are unique. We don't need to be perfect. We can be perfectly imperfect and that is fine. What is perfection to one is imperfection to another.

But underlying both these thoughts is something else. Slow down . . . breathe . . . and just be still. Who is aware of the breath? Who is thinking 'I am not good enough'? There is an 'I' that just is, existing as pure awareness beneath all thoughts and feelings. Isn't this also yourself? When the self that thinks I am not good enough meets the self that just is, perfection is achieved. This self needs no acceptance. Willingness to accept is willingness to meet this self in its purity and perfection. Instead of saying 'I accept myself as I am' (implying flaws and all) we can also say 'I accept that I am', and that is enough. In this way, we are always good enough because we exist.

Accepting others

Once we have accepted ourselves with all our imperfections, we can extend this acceptance to others. We have all encountered behaviour we don't like in others. It is the behaviour that is in error if it hurts someone. When we become disconnected from our wholeness, it is the fragmented aspect of ourselves that is capable of causing pain to another person.

We can choose not to interact with people whose behaviour we don't like. Accepting another human being means we make this choice with a peaceful heart. We accept what we like and what we don't like. How we relate to them is another matter. We can choose to distance ourselves from people who are not harmonious with us. With acceptance, we distance without judgement or blame. We let them be who they are and then respond according to our preferences. In this way, our inner peace remains undisturbed.

Ultimate acceptance is allowing yourself to experience life as it is without resistance. We don't have to like it and often we won't like it at all. We can honestly express our dislike and allow ourselves to feel that too. This is part of what's happening. No need to deny it. No need to resist. The amount of resistance you have will be equal to the

level of stress and suffering you experience. The important
questions to ask yourself are:

- How will I respond?
- What experience do I choose to have?
- What outcome do I want to create?

Accepting the unacceptable

When something as big as a terrorist attack explodes into
your life, there is no choice but to accept it because it takes
over every emotion and thought, as well as the physical
reality of one's life, which is now changed forever. Death
has taken over, so what is left? My sons and I were in
Florida when my Alan and Naomi were crouched under a
table at the Tiffin restaurant (now renamed Fenix) in the
Oberoi. Our lives were never threatened and yet life as we
knew it ended at the snap of a bullet. In Mumbai, the family
and friends of those who were killed in the attack were also
confronted with this experience. I read articles about how
the city snapped back into action to clean up the mess,
grieve the loss of lives and find ways to increase security.
There were many heroes that emerged from this tragedy.
Some of their stories are captured in an *Indian Express* book
titled *26/11: Stories of Strength*. I read about 'the spirit of
Mumbai' and felt inspired to experience it for myself; I was
eager to meet some of these people when the time was right.

I learnt that the only way to accept the unacceptable
is to accept life itself—to embrace it fully and without
reserve, to learn to live with love no matter what. Love
never dies, and that is what life offers in every moment,

even in the worst moments of our lives. This kind of acceptance is an ongoing process. It hits me harder as each year passes. Life does move on, but our memories remain and move along with it. I have come to see that living with this experience is ultimate acceptance. Acceptance is not passive; I cannot walk away and say 'well, that's over now'. This is now an intimate part of my life that has dramatically changed who I am. My acceptance is living with it, not against it.

Everyday acceptance

Every day, life presents us with experiences that we like and don't like—anything from the weather, traffic and meals to conversations with family, friends and co-workers, to challenging situations, unexpected obstacles or pleasant surprises.

I remember receiving a message from my sister Lorrie one day in December 2010 during my first trip to Mumbai. It was not good news. Our mother had just been diagnosed with stage four lung cancer and would require chemotherapy beginning in January. I had been planning to stay on in Mumbai to work on an Interfaith peace project with students from St Andrews College, but I was needed in Florida. My sister worked, and her schedule did not enable her to handle driving to doctor's appointments and all that would be required to assist our mother during this time. I had to accept this situation and return to Florida in January after the Interfaith symposium on forgiveness, where I was scheduled to speak. I needed to put Mumbai on hold.

Journal entry, 20 January 2011

I must let go of resistance to what is happening and accept reality. The reality today is my mother is alive. She is not dying. She is living. She doesn't want to accept death and why should she? The chemo treatments may turn things around if enough cancer cells are destroyed. She can still dress herself, and if I help her into the bathroom, she can sit on a special chair in the shower and wash herself. She's very happy about that. She has accepted this situation with grace. Have I accepted this situation? This is my focus for the day—acceptance.

As I endeavoured to be more accepting of my mother's situation, I was challenged to be accepting of the history of our family life over the years, my relationship with my parents, my brothers and sister, and the fact that I was now on my own. I had not spent much time with them in recent years as we were spread out in various parts of the United States. Now that our mother was possibly dying, everyone gathered for more visits. Memories of our childhood were shared amid laughter and appreciation for having this intimate time with Mom. But within all of this, we slowly began to accept the possible end of her life.

We don't like to think life will ever end. Dying of cancer is slow-motion death. Alan and Naomi died abruptly, much sooner than would be expected. Alan was fifty-eight, Naomi only thirteen. My mother was only seventy-two and felt she had more years to live, and in fact, stated that she was not dying. We hoped she was right. In the meantime, cancer was a reality we had to accept, along with the treatment required with no guaranteed outcome. I surrendered to this situation with acceptance and was able to enjoy the simple moments of each day. Nothing much was happening other than that, but this 'nothing much' was full of precious moments containing tenderness and love.

I observed many moments of tenderness on the streets of Mumbai when I was there. Many people had to accept the pavement as their dwelling place. As the endless traffic streamed by, their lives were in full view for all who cared to observe. Entire families slept, ate, worked and played on their section of pavement. I remember thinking, as the black and yellow taxi slowly crept past in the morning rush hour, 'They don't look depressed or hopeless at all. They look content.' Children were playing games, mothers were making tea and chapatis and a father was pouring a bucket of soapy water over his head for his morning bath. This was ordinary life for them. It was said that if a person arrived in Mumbai without a rupee in his pocket, he could be working that very day and would eat that night. These people would accept whatever work was available or would begin making and selling crafts on the street. I knew it wasn't so simple for a lot of them, but I did see many more smiles than frowns. I heard laughter and songs amidst the heavy traffic every single day. These people demonstrated the 'spirit of Mumbai' I had heard so much about. I saw this spirit in every city I visited in India.

Putting acceptance into practice

The first step is to set your inner compass to acceptance and to create an affirmative intention you can say to yourself such as:

> Today I am willing to accept things as they are. I accept
> myself as I am. I accept others as they are. I am grateful
> for the experience of acceptance and the peace that it
> brings me.

If this feels unnatural or challenging, you can turn it into a
prayer. Prayer is an intimate way to connect to the divine
within as you open your heart, share your challenges and
ask for help to understand and resolve what is lacking.
I have often used a simple prayer to the divine, such as:

> Dear God, help me to accept what is happening. I don't
> like it, but I can't change it. Help me to move forward
> with this and make the best of it.

To strengthen this focus, write it down and read it aloud.
Then close your eyes for a few minutes as you let it sink
into your consciousness. Take a few deep breaths and allow
any resistance to melt away.

It is helpful to keep a journal to note challenges and
insights about your experience of practising acceptance.
This will reveal patterns you may not have noticed before
and help you to let go of resistance. In this simple way,
you will begin to experience the benefits of becoming more
accepting of the daily happenings of life as they arise.

You can strengthen any positive aspect of your life by
making a conscious choice to do so. Self-acceptance is key
to self-love. Can you accept your humanity as well as your
divinity? Each of us contains both. The divinity is harder to
find, but it's there and will reveal itself when called upon.
I have found this to be true over and over again. This is the

true security blanket that will always comfort me when I feel untethered and alone. When I allow myself to accept the divine within, I am embraced by a love that never fails me, never leaves me, never dies, never changes its mind and wanders off. We each contain a love so deep and vast it is invisible, yet so near.

We are body, mind, emotions and spirit, all interacting with each other to process our life experiences. Accept yourself as you are and accept your experience as it is. We can't change something that happened, but we can choose how we respond and how we act in relation to that experience.

We can direct our thoughts to the experiences we choose to have. Choice is the keyword here—you have a choice to direct your thoughts and change your entire perspective and, therefore, your experience. If you want to experience the peace of mind that acceptance will bring, make that your intention for the day. This will bring a state of balance. From a balanced state of heart and mind you will be able to take the most appropriate actions to fulfil your day. This is true power—the power of love in action.

May this day be filled with acceptance of yourself and others and may acceptance fill your heart with peace. Remember to accept the beauty inside yourself as well as the beauty hiding beneath the surface in others.

5

Deep Listening

'So when you are listening to somebody, completely, attentively, then you are listening not only to the words, but also to the feeling of what is being conveyed, to the whole of it, not part of it.'—Jiddu Krishnamurti

We hear sounds all day long, but how often do we really listen?

Deep listening requires a willingness to listen with an open heart and mind. Listening with acceptance invites honest sharing of thoughts and feelings. Slow down and just sit still. Be open to what is being said to you without the need to interrupt. Listen without judgement or resistance. Just listen. How often do we listen to the feelings beneath the words? Listening with silent presence is a precious gift we give to the person speaking. It sounds simple, but it is deceptively challenging. Thoughts distract from the act of listening deeply, leading our minds on all kinds of tangents. It takes practice to listen deeply, but it is well worth the effort when insights, understanding and intimate connections increase as a result.

Why are we so good at judging? Judgements put up a wall that prevents us from listening and connecting from the heart. The way to break the habit of judging is to simply notice it and learn to ignore the judgements. When we don't give our attention to judgements, they shrink back into our minds and allow our minds to open and listen deeply.

I remember watching a news interview on television. Two people were talking back and forth, often interrupting and then speaking over each other. There was no sharing of ideas or deepening of understanding of the issue being discussed. In this case, it was about the politics of the day. There was no intention to listen, only to speak and make a case for a particular point of view. In the end, nothing was gained by either side, nor were the viewers educated in a balanced way.

I have also seen interviews on various subjects where the interviewer gave full attention to the interviewee after posing a question. This elicited thoughtful responses that gave rise to more sharing and insightful comments. Each of them learnt a lot from each other about the subject under discussion. As a viewer, I was exposed to an enriching conversation that I could continue to reflect upon. Simi Garewal is a deep listener and it is why her talk show is so popular in India—she listens with full attention, combined with acceptance. This makes people feel safe and opens them to sharing what is in their hearts and souls. As we listen to intimate sharing, we learn something about ourselves as we gain a deeper understanding of life.

It's often challenging to be a good listener. We want to say what we need to say and get on with it. I've been guilty of rushing my thoughts forward in a conversation and not taking the time to fully listen. True listening is an art that takes a lot of practise and is well worth the effort. It is as much a gift to ourselves as it is to others.

Journal entry, January 2011, Florida

Today, I will listen carefully and completely so that all the information I need is fully heard. I will listen with my heart as well as my mind.

Listening requires slowing down and ignoring other thoughts that interrupt the process of paying attention. My mother isn't talking much, so I listen to the silence between the words and the ordinary sounds of doing dishes, coffee percolating, cooking, laundry, morning birds. There is a deeper listening if I pay attention to the tone of voice, what is said, what is not being said, sighs of exasperation, chuckles in response to whatever someone said on the phone when they called to say hi. First thing in the morning, I listen for Mom to get out of bed and then I go out to get the newspaper from the driveway and turn on the coffee, so it is ready by the time she walks slowly out to the kitchen. I feel comforted by this routine. After Alan and Naomi died, I no longer had a routine that involved other people. I missed that. I am in the process of getting to know myself in a brand new way. I am also getting to know my mother, not so much through what is being talked about, but by sharing these routines each day. The sound of my mother's voice hasn't changed much since I was a child. She was always a good listener, but I sometimes get too excited when I share something I care passionately about and forget to listen. There is a lot I would love to ask her, but in the silence I can sense that questions would not be welcome. She wants to carry on with her routines, enjoy the days when she has the strength to sit up. She is living in the present moment, day by day. So I listen to my inner voice telling me to be quiet and just focus on the tasks of the day without commentary or reflection about what it all means.

As I engaged in this practice, I felt a deeper connection to my mother and knew that listening in this way was just as important as having a conversation about everyday matters.

If we're not listening fully, our experience is half-lived. We miss receiving what another person is offering through their communication. Listening is essential to meaningful relationships, whether personal or professional. True connection that leads to a deeper understanding and acceptance of what the person is communicating will take us beyond the superficial aspects of a relationship.

There are many levels of listening. Let's begin with ourselves.

How can we listen to ourselves? Unless we have learnt to listen to our own inner voice, we cannot expect to listen with full attention to another person. We are multi-dimensional human beings comprised of body, mind, emotions and spirit. Self-listening in each of these dimensions will keep us tuned in to what is happening within us so that we can make the best choices for ourselves.

Begin with the body—how does the body speak to us? The body lets us know all kinds of things about how it is feeling moment by moment. It tells us when it is tired, hungry, hot, cold, anxious, sad, happy, calm, afraid or excited. If we listen to our body, it will give us our personal barometer reading for the day.

The mind is full of thoughts. What are your thoughts telling you? What stories are going on in your mind? What or who are you judging? What are you commenting on moment to moment? Our thoughts speak to us of what we care about, what we fear, what we resist and what excites us. There are patterns of thoughts that reveal our obsessions, attachments and priorities. There is much to learn about ourselves just by observing our thoughts.

Our emotions are often felt in our bodies and play out in the way we think about life's happenings. Feelings are more subtle and are more intuitive, a trustworthy barometer to guide us throughout our challenges in life.

Emotions are reactions to thoughts and situations that occur. Emotions are often based on our interpretation of what has occurred. This is where it is worthwhile to listen closely and ask questions before jumping to conclusions.

Our inner voice will speak to us through our thoughts and feelings. Our spiritual centre is felt in silence. In silence, we can tune in to the source of our being. Silence may not have a sound, but it does have a presence. Listening to this presence is felt rather than heard.

Everyday listening

When I first arrived in Mumbai, I was bombarded with new sounds, sounds that happened every day on the streets there that I had not encountered before. I remember hearing drums and bells often. There were so many celebrations, both religious holidays and weddings, that filled the streets with music, chanting, drums and bells.

And of course, the dominating sound on the streets of Mumbai was the honking of horns in traffic. Every hour of the day was packed with traffic going in all directions. The honking never ceased. Sometimes you could hear a traffic cop's whistle blowing as he tried to keep things moving. For some reason, the drivers were convinced that honking would move things along. It never did, but the honking continued anyway. People got used to it as a normal part of everyday life in this bustling city.

I now live on the other side of the world, far from a big city. I live in the middle of a 400-acre forest in a meditation sanctuary. This environment is as opposite as can be from Mumbai. I love the contrast of India, but when it was time to recharge my inner batteries, I was grateful to return to the silence of the trees. The sounds I hear in this place are birds, rustling leaves, wind, rain and the occasional conversations I have with the other sanctuary residents. We are a meditative group of people, so we don't feel the need to chat all the time. We often eat in silence. This is a place where one's own thoughts dominate. It is so silent here that I have a lot of practice listening to my thoughts. I have learnt to ignore thoughts that obsess on the past, or thoughts that twist events into negative stories. Release and let go is often my daily mantra in this quiet place for retreat and renewal. When we declutter our minds, something new can be born, a new you can emerge.

Listening to the past

The past can teach us a lot about who we were and give us insights into what we have learnt from our previous experiences, both positive and negative. To listen to the past, simply sit quietly with your eyes closed. Breathe deeply a few times, and as you feel more relaxed, inquire within yourself, 'Is there anything I need to release from the past?' If nothing comes up in the next few moments, that's fine. If memories come up, just watch and notice how you feel. Accept whatever comes up without judgement. Just observe and accept with gratitude for the learning it brought you. Whatever happened is over now, and you are in this moment, not in the past. Who you are today is the result of your entire history. What comes before you is a huge white canvas waiting to be painted with any colours you choose.

To listen or not to listen . . .

Do negative thoughts serve a purpose? What are they trying to tell us? We can learn a lot from our thoughts. They tell us what we think is most important. Is it? If we think about someone or some situation all the time, is that what matters most? Is that what we value most? Does it serve us to give so much attention to those thoughts? Is there still something to be learnt or is it time to let go? These questions are worth reflection and contemplation. Discernment is needed. It is worth taking the time to reflect and decide how you want to move forward. Are actions needed or is it best to do nothing and say nothing at this time? This is where listening to your inner self is valuable. Other people will be happy and even eager to tell you what they think, but only you can know what is best for you.

There are times when negative thoughts occupy our minds in the form of judgements on ourselves and others. Judgements and criticism will disconnect us from our heart, from the source of our being and thus separate us from our world. Distance ensues and then doors shut tight, disallowing communication and sharing. Without truthful communication, there will be no opportunity for harmonious resolution.

We cannot control our thoughts, but we can control our attention to our thoughts. We can choose not to let certain thoughts influence our speech and actions. Take the time to notice what thoughts are coming up, question whether these thoughts have truth or require further reflection. Notice what feelings arise in you along with those thoughts. You can choose not to listen to thoughts that will harm you or others. If those thoughts do not serve your health and well-being, let them dissolve into the ocean of your being. You have the power of choice to redirect your thoughts. You do not need to be held hostage by negative thoughts. I like to imagine tossing such thoughts into a deep well and then pulling up fresh water to cleanse my mind.

Meditative listening

Practise listening to your inner self by sitting still and bringing your attention to your heart as you breathe. Close your eyes and just be. You can then simply ask your inner being, 'Is there anything I need to know about this situation?' 'What is the truth about this?' 'How should I act in relation to it?' These questions will prompt the wisdom of the heart to come forth. After a few moments, write down whatever comes to you.

Deep listening requires full attention—not only to the words but to the feelings beneath the words.

Listen to the world around you that is beyond words. Listen to life in all its glory and all its madness.

When you bring your full attention to listening, what do you hear? What do you feel? All the sounds we hear in a day combine to create the tapestry of our lives.

Listening is another way to receive the gift of life. Listening to the heart will open us to our innate wisdom—our most trusted guide.

Listening is an important step towards forgiveness. We listen so that we may learn about what happened, what was the motivation and why. In the case of the Mumbai terrorist attack, my family and I listened to the news. That's all we had for information. We listened, but that did not change the result. But for forgiveness to bring us back to a state of balance from where we can then move forward with our lives, we must listen to the story. Forgiveness is not about agreement or avoiding the impact of an act that hurt us deeply.

One of the most powerful examples that I know of on how listening led to forgiveness is the story of Jo Berry and Patrick Magee.

Jo Berry's father, Sir Anthony Barry, a Tory Member of Parliament, was killed in the Brighton hotel bombing of 1984. Patrick Magee was the IRA man who planted the bomb. I had a chance to hear Jo Berry tell her story with Patrick Magee at a peace conference that I attended in Oxford, England, in 2015. When Patrick Magee was released from prison as part of the Good Friday agreement thirteen years after the bombing, Jo Berry arranged to meet him. She said she wanted to understand why he did what he did. So she asked the question and she listened. And then he listened to her story. At the end of three hours, something had changed in each of them. They saw each other not as the enemy but as human beings. By listening attentively to each other they gained an understanding that went beyond politics and justifications and blame. In the end, Jo Berry said there was nothing to forgive because she felt such empathy for the human being Patrick Magee, who was fighting a struggle he believed in, a struggle where the two sides had demonized each other to the extent they could never sit down and listen. As a result, there was much violence and hundreds of people were killed in both England and Ireland over many years. Jo Berry and Patrick Magee now speak together all over the world to promote peace through the charity Jo founded, Building Bridges for Peace. No longer a terrorist, Patrick Magee is now a peace activist.

Listening is a key ingredient to moving towards peace and reconciliation. This is true in every relationship, both personal and political.

Listening is a choice that will lead to understanding, forgiveness and peace.

When it's time to listen, slow down, smile in acknowledgment, take a deep breath and give your full attention to the person in front of you who is taking the time to share their thoughts and feelings. True listening will bring a deeper connection to yourself, your relationships and to life itself.

6

Speaking the Truth

'The truth is such a rare thing, it is delightful to tell it.'—Emily Dickinson

Speaking the truth is about truthful communication—no frills honesty. To speak the truth, you must know your truth. What is true for you may not be true for someone else. Once you have listened with careful attention, you can discern the truth regarding yourself and others as you discover ways to express your truth. Here is what I wrote in my journal as I was exploring this practice for myself:

Today I will say what I mean and mean what I say. I will be direct, with respect. I will be clear in my communication as I speak with kindness and compassion. Speaking the truth means being honest and so much more. It means being clear and direct, speaking from the heart and soul. There is so much being written and spoken about 'living your truth' and 'speaking your truth'. Is there any such thing as 'the' truth? The only truth I know for sure is that I exist. I am here. What else is going on? All that is filtered through my consciousness, which includes my individual perceptions about the world around me.

I have a lifelong habit of not speaking up for myself. There are a lot of things I choose not to share with my dying mother for fear of imposing on her solitude. I also fear annoying her with questions or comments. What would I share with her now if I could? I know there is a time limit and at some point in time my mother will make her transition from this life. I know that means when she dies, but I am not experiencing her as 'dying'. Her physical life is fading away, that's for sure. I can see it diminishing day by day. Maybe it is the chemo treatment that is taking away her energy and her radiance. We all want to believe the chemo will save her. It has saved other people and many people survive lung cancer, so why not our mother? Was it too late? In my heart I feel this is it, that it is the end for her, it is only a matter of a few more months. I don't know if this is true, so I will not speak this out. I feel guilty for thinking this, and I want to be optimistic. I want to keep thinking her recovery is possible, and so I will open myself to that attitude and help her to be as comfortable as we can make her. Right now, I will speak what I think is the truth silently and will not say any of this out loud.

To speak the truth is to be aligned with our true nature. To speak truthfully, we must know ourselves from the inside out. Our highest truth is in our hearts. When we speak from the heart, we are speaking the truth. That is all we really need to know. But this is easier said than done.

We may know the truth about a situation or feel strongly about something but speaking it out may bring fear. Facing this fear is the first step. You can simply wait for the fear to subside, but if strong feelings continue to come up, it is time to speak it out. It helps to write it out first, without any edits or deletions, in the privacy of your own space. When we develop clarity on the situation, we can determine if it is appropriate to speak the truth outwardly to someone or simply acknowledge the truth within ourselves. In this way, we come to a harmonious resolution. In this way, speaking the truth brings us peace. If we expect forgiveness from others, we must share our truth. If we expect to heal from a loss, we must listen to our thoughts and communicate what needs to be shared to move forward.

I remember having a recurring thought that I wanted to travel to Mumbai to see for myself where Alan and Naomi had spent the last ten days of their lives. I wanted to meet the staff at the Oberoi hotel and hear their stories about what had happened during the terrorist attack. I wanted to meet Mr P.R.S. Oberoi and invite him to share in our vision of creating a message of peace, love and compassion in response to an act of hatred and violence. How to go about making all this happen? I was petrified at the thought. But I was also compelled to push forward. And so, after a couple of emails and a phone call with Mr Oberoi himself, I found myself on a plane to India with one of the survivors from our group—first to Delhi to meet Mr Oberoi and then to Mumbai to meet the head staff of the Oberoi hotel.

The meeting with Mr Oberoi was scheduled for 3 p.m. on Sunday, 4 July. I kept thinking, 'What will I say? How will I say it?' I had never met with someone so high up in the business world. And this wasn't just any successful businessman. He was the owner of the hotel where my husband and daughter were killed.

Mr Oberoi arrived looking elegant in a grey silk suit. He offered me tea and asked if I would mind if he lit up his cigar. He opened the meeting by saying, 'I'm sorry about the deaths of your husband and daughter. We also lost many long-time staff members who were like family to us.'

I began by telling him about all the emails we had received from around the world and how this had inspired us to continue sharing the message of peace, love and compassion that had been extended to us in the aftermath of the attack. 'I can't let their deaths go to waste,' I told him. 'We must do something to create a positive outcome to this tragedy. I refuse to be held hostage by the terrorists.'

I described our vision for One Life Alliance, a non-profit initiative we were creating to engage people in the conversation about the oneness and sacredness of the life we all share. Our intention was to create a positive focus that could be applied in daily life. The more people became involved, the more we could prevent acts of terror by creating acts of love.

Mr Oberoi nodded in agreement as he smoked his cigar and the peacock outside fanned his tail feathers. 'Business has been slow since the attacks, and we don't know how long it will take for things to pick up, so I can't offer you funds, but I can offer accommodations for your visits and for the members of your group to attend the launch in Mumbai.'

I was moved by his generosity and thoughtfulness. 'Thank you so much. That will be so helpful.' He proceeded to give me his personal mobile number and said I could call him any time for advice. He was true to his word. I never saw him again, but from 2010 to 2016, I stayed at the Trident Hotel in Mumbai for over one thousand nights. For each visit, I sent a request by email, and each time, it was approved by Mr Oberoi himself.

Pushing through my initial fear of speaking my truth to a powerful man opened many doors that led to more opportunities to speak and share this important truth. Mr Oberoi recognized this truth and was willing to provide an important way to make it possible to share it with thousands more from all over the world. I am forever grateful for this act of love.

Practise speaking the truth

Begin with writing down and then reading aloud these statements of intention:

- Today, I will speak truthfully in every conversation. Truth is integrity.
- I use my words to express the truth of who I am and what life is for me.
- As I am truthful, I am respecting myself and others.
- I speak the truth with love and compassion.

We are most truthful when we speak from the heart. When we speak from the heart, we bring the power of peace to our world. Sit still for a few minutes as you read over your statements of intention. Let these statements rest in your heart with love and gratitude for the opportunity to share your truth. What is your truth in this moment? Take a few moments to slow down, reflect and write what comes to you without censoring or editing. What truth do you wish to share with yourself? Sacred truths are revealed in quiet moments when we are open to receiving.

7

Understanding with an Open Heart

'Understanding can overcome any situation, however mysterious or insurmountable it may appear to be.'—Norman Vincent Peale

Acceptance, listening and speaking truthfully will naturally lead to an increased understanding of yourself and others, a key ingredient to forgiveness. Understanding is to gain insight into the truth of a matter as well as what has been misunderstood or misinterpreted. And crucially, it is also the ability to discern between these two—truth and non-truth. Being grounded in the truth of who you are gives rise to discernment. This, in turn, brings the possibility of inner and outer peace.

To strengthen understanding, it is helpful to approach each encounter with a willingness to understand with an open heart and mind. Ask questions and listen deeply before offering your response and jumping to conclusions. Even if you will never agree with a person, you can come to understand the underlying causes for their actions. When this happens, forgiveness becomes possible.

My reflections on understanding—my intention: I will be open to understanding more deeply today—understanding what? Understanding what is needed so I can make the best decisions possible and serve my friends and family most effectively. I will first understand all parts of a situation and then take the most appropriate action. That means asking a lot more questions.

And I suppose it means letting go of the need to understand. There are some things I will never understand. Why did Alan and Naomi have to be killed in a terrorist attack? Why did those young men feel the need to kill all those people? Why did the controllers giving instructions to them do what they did? What did they think it would accomplish and for what purpose? This is beyond my understanding. In this case, I must accept even though I do not understand. This is more challenging. Understanding yields acceptance. When I understand something, I accept it, I appreciate the purpose of it even though I might not agree with it.

In addition to asking more questions, understanding requires deep listening. When I listen with an intent to understand, the questions that emerge will help this process.

Life throws questions at us that may never be answered. In order to have peace, we can choose to accept reality and let go of the need to understand. If not, we will live with frustration and resentment. I choose to live in peace. Therefore, I choose to forgive. I do my best to understand, and then I let go and accept the way things came to pass. Forgiveness is then possible. It doesn't mean I will like something or agree with it. But I accept it. I am still here, I am alive and I want to give forth something that will be of value. I cannot do this in a state of anger or judgement. What I can do is transmute the anger to positive energy that fuels my passion to bring peace, compassion and love into this world.

Misunderstanding leads to disconnection. When we don't understand, we create distance between ourselves and others. This distance can be bridged with a willingness to understand or at least accept that which cannot be understood. Understanding may come over time or in an instant. But it will never come if we put up barriers in our hearts and minds. The possibility of understanding begins with opening the heart and mind. Understanding leads to peace.

Sometime in the summer of 2008, a Pakistani family visited the Synchronicity Sanctuary in Virginia, where we were resident staff members. Mohammed Alam and his wife Naila, along with her sister and a few others, arrived in a van to tour the property and increase their understanding about Synchronicity Meditation as a tool to create inner and outer peace. My daughter Naomi had made a fresh batch of almond cookies to serve with tea before we piled into golf carts to drive along the mountain path. It was the first time I had ever met people from Pakistan. They now lived in northern Virginia with extended family members. It was inspiring to talk with them and learn about their vision for world peace. This was my first understanding of what it means to be Muslim.

A few months later, the Mumbai terrorist attack happened. The terrorists were young Pakistani men of Islamic faith, who had spent many months training for this attack. One of the first email messages we received in the aftermath of the terrorist attack was from an Iranian Muslim. 'Islam means peace. We send you our love and our prayers.' I was grateful for this loving message of peace.

Because of these connections, I felt it was important to invite Mohammed and Naila Alam to Alan and Naomi's memorial service and ask if they would say a few words. Mohammed was travelling in Pakistan at the time, so Naila and her sister Yasmin attended. Naila spoke and shared a compassionate message from the then Pakistani ambassador to the United States, Mr Husain Haqqani:

> Please accept our heartfelt condolence at this unfortunate demise of your loved ones at the Mumbai attack. Such despicable and shameless attacks are condemned by Pakistanis all over the world. May God help you in this difficult time to gain strength and fortitude to bear this irreplaceable loss.

Naila and I became friends and continue to remain in touch. I reached out to her on Naomi's birthday in 2010, on 3 February. She invited me to her home in northern Virginia and insisted I stay overnight so that she could introduce me to the local imam and some of her friends. I will never forget that visit. We took a photo of Alan and Naomi to show the imam when I told him the story of what had happened. He looked at it for a long time and then tears filled his eyes and rolled down into his beard. He shook his head and said, 'This should not have happened, this should not have happened.' As we were leaving, Naila told me that in her culture, men did not cry, and so the imam's reaction was very unusual. The tears of the imam showed empathy and understanding of the heartbreaking loss of human lives.

That night the dinner in Naila's home was a full-scale family celebration with four generations all living in the same large townhouse. It was a delicious feast with an array of spicy Pakistani food. They gave me a gorgeous embroidered woollen shawl from Pakistan, and as we said our goodbyes, the grandmother pointed to the front door and said to me, 'This door is your door, and this door will always be open to you.' I was so moved by their generosity and loving embrace of someone they had met for the first time. I felt surrounded by love and friendship. I knew Alan and Naomi would be pleased. I gained an understanding that differences in religious beliefs are on the surface and what is most important is the connections of hearts.

Practising the art of understanding

Begin this process by stating these intentions to strengthen your focus on understanding:

- Here and now, I am open to increasing understanding of myself and others.
- I am willing to understand in all situations. I am accepting and contributing peace to my world.

- Understanding softens my heart and opens my mind.
- As I understand, I am honouring myself and those in my world.
- Understanding leads to truth. Understanding leads to love and forgiveness. Understanding leads to connection.

Here are some reflective questions to assist you to increase your understanding of yourself and others. Understand yourself to gain insight that will lead to understanding others.

As you open yourself to increasing your understanding of yourself and others, what in your life requires more understanding?

What would it take to increase your understanding?

Do you need to ask more questions?

Do you need to share your understanding with someone?

Did increasing your understanding enable you to resolve a conflict?

The big question for me is, 'What have I come to understand about life?'

True understanding comes from experience. I can understand myself by experiencing all aspects of myself fully—from the inside out. Meditation helped me connect to the source within. I experienced the source of my being— pure silence, emptiness, infinite space of awareness, awake and alive. The extent to which I remain connected to this source is the extent to which I feel connected to other people and the world around me. The more connected I am, the more loving I am. Love flows into my life through my words and actions.

Love wants to give forth of itself without holding back. I understand that love never dies. The death of a human body does not kill the love that human experienced nor does it kill the love that friends and family of that human had for them. Things die and people die but love remains. This is the most precious understanding—that life is sacred because it contains love. Life is made of love. Love will provide what is needed when we allow love into our experience. It is not outside of us. But when we shut down our hearts and close our minds, love cannot flow through us. When love cannot flow, we suffer. This is when we feel most separated from life. If we don't understand what is causing this feeling of separation, we look outside ourselves to blame others.

When there is a disconnection from self, there is a disconnection from life and love. The extent to which I am disconnected is the extent to which I am capable of harming another person. The need to cause pain is born of disconnection from the life and love within ourselves. In the extreme, this enables a disconnected person to commit acts of terror, violence and death.

The ultimate connection is living in unity with life, flowing in harmony with the way things are. Feeling at one with ourselves and with all of life is the highest form of love, a sacred love emerging from an open heart.

8

Forgiveness Is Possible

'Each act of forgiveness is a drop of water in a bucket. With every drop comes a splash, sending ripples of non-violence and positivity. After enough drops, the bucket is full, leaving no room for hate.'—Aaron John Butler, Naomi's brother

So far in this book, we have been creating a path that brings us to the possibility of forgiveness, or at least creates a willingness to consider this choice. Understanding true forgiveness is a personal process. This process takes place within your heart. For me, this is a process of choosing to remain connected to the source of love within.

My response to the death of my husband and daughter includes forgiveness. This does not mean pardon, nor does it mean condoning a despicable action, or not holding a person accountable for cold-blooded murder. Forgiveness is a personal choice to accept what cannot be changed, however hurtful. Forgiveness has nothing to do with the terrorist. I have no personal relationship with that terrorist, other than we are both human beings. Do I want to hold on to anger, resentment, feelings of revenge and retaliation? According to St Augustine, this is 'like taking poison and hoping your enemy dies'.

Forgiveness allows me to keep my heart open so that I can continue to love the life I'm now living. This is how I choose to honour the memory of Alan and Naomi. I have chosen to create a living memorial that brings the possibility of peace, compassion and love to this world. This is what gives me purpose and allows me to keep living, to keep loving, and to open myself to a greater vision for humanity that could create an environment for positive change.

This would mean a society where life is valued above all else. This would mean a major transformation of priorities for most of the world. This is another kind of 'climate change'. We could create a climate of mutual love and respect, which forms the foundation of another way to evaluate our conflicts and resolve our differences. It would mean collaborating in new ways and communicating truthfully with an intention to work things out with integrity.

I know this sounds utopian, but I believe we can move in this direction—to honour the sacredness of this life we share, to live it, breathe it and celebrate it.

Slow down, smile, take a deep breath . . . be more accepting of the differences around you, listen more fully, speak the truth with respect, be willing to understand a different view, forgive, forgive and forgive some more. This is love.

Love is compassionate and love forgives. Therefore, I choose love. Love is the opposite of terrorism. If any human being on this planet is suffering, their connection to love is lacking. Love will provide what is needed most in every corner of this earth. We can each be more loving in a thousand different ways. If I can be more loving by forgiving the terrorist who killed my husband and my daughter, I can start living again. Now I can renew my life, a life that does not include Alan and Naomi. But it does include the love for them that will never die. Why else are we here if not to love? Without love, what is the point? When Alan and Naomi were killed, love remained. When my mother died of lung cancer, love remained. A part of me died with each of their deaths, but love remained. Love is the core ingredient of this human life. Love is our greatest natural resource. There is no end to love unless we close the door to our hearts.

Forgiveness applied to the world of business

For this message to have a practical and tangible impact, I knew it must be applied in business, education and government. And so I continued making multiple trips to Mumbai and eventually England as well so that I could connect with people in various sectors of society. I was also making new friends from these countries and I felt invigorated by living in different environments where I had no personal past to haunt me.

One of the gifts that came forth as I travelled to India and England was the opportunity to meet people from the business world. I was surprised and delighted to discover that people in the business world in India were open to views on the subject of forgiveness. It's not something that normally comes up in conversation, but once I shared the reason why I was in Mumbai it would inevitably include a discussion about forgiveness. A British businessman I met at an India Business Group meeting had some interesting things to say on the subject. In an email he shared his views on forgiveness in the world of business, showing that forgiveness has a role to play in everyday life, both personal and professional.

From Nigel Lang, a businessman operating in UK and Mumbai:

The importance of forgiveness in the world of business:

I can think of numerous real examples where forgiveness in business has reaped tangible rewards and plenty of examples where vindictive lack of forgiveness has cost companies dear. I make it a very strong principle of my companies' culture that we do not have witch hunts, we do not hold grudges and we do get on with looking forward. Too many opportunities are lost by bearing grudges and too much energy is wasted trying to beat the enemy. There is no place for enemies in business and no place for any emotion other than love:

· Love of life
· Love of people
· Love of satisfying needs
· Love of a happy customer
· Love of a challenge
· Love of creativity
· Love of organization

· Love of teamwork
· Love of planning
· Love of promotion
· Love of individuality
· Love of teaching
· Love of growth
· Love of fairness
· Love of equality
· Love of fulfilment
· Love of abundance

That my dear, is why forgiveness is so important even in the simple world of business!

I had the privilege of meeting Nigel's ninety-year-old father the following year in England, and he was happy to share with me his views on forgiveness.

'Forgiveness is the key to harmony.
Forgiveness is the antidote to hurt.
Forgiveness is love in action.
Forgiveness is the lubricant of a contented life.
Forgiveness and hate are incompatible.
Forgiveness is the power of reconciliation.
Forgiveness breeds forgiveness.
Love breeds forgiveness breeds love breeds forgiveness.'
—*Michael Lang from Canterbury, England*

As you can see, there is much worth contemplating with regard to forgiveness. Both Nigel and his father demonstrated that forgiveness is an essential ingredient not only for success in business but also for one's inner peace. Forgiveness is an act of love we give to ourselves once we understand the value of this powerful practice.

While in London in 2019, I attended an inspiring annual event hosted by The Forgiveness Project.

'The Forgiveness Project collects and shares stories from both victims/survivors and perpetrators of crime and conflict who have rebuilt their lives following hurt and trauma.

Founded in 2004 by journalist Marina Cantacuzino, The Forgiveness Project provides resources and experiences to help people examine and overcome their own unresolved grievances. The testimonies we collect bear witness to the resilience of the human spirit and act as a powerful antidote to narratives of hate and dehumanization, presenting alternatives to cycles of conflict, violence, crime and injustice.' (From www.theforgivenessproject.com)

Founder Marina Cantacuzino's keynote speech at the event stated very clearly the importance of forgiveness:

'I have never wanted the stories we share to simplify or sanctify forgiveness. I don't want to express forgiveness as something just for the mentally strong or the morally superior. And I know it must never be prescribed because if you make forgiveness a duty, it can easily become a tyranny.

'The stories shared by The Forgiveness Project express the process of forgiveness differently. For some it is sudden, for others it takes decades; for some it emerges quietly from the depths of their being, for others it may be prompted by a single encounter or event. For some it depends on an apology (making amends), for others it is entirely unconditional and an act of self-healing.'

The importance of sharing the stories of forgiveness is clearly demonstrated by people who place a high value on how intimately we are all connected. As Marina so beautifully said, there are many ways to forgive, many understandings of what forgiveness is and no timeline for forgiveness. It is a personal process that is unique for each of us.

Two examples of personal healing as a result of forgiveness were shared with me by two young women in Mumbai who were students at the Don Bosco school in Matunga and had attended a peace rally where I was invited to share my story of forgiveness. I spoke at Don Bosco again a year later where one of the students approached me and said that forgiveness had saved her life. She then proceeded to tell me that her brother had been sexually abusing her and she had planned to commit suicide. After the peace rally the year before, she had decided she would forgive her brother to free herself from inner turmoil. As a result, the situation resolved itself and she was free of further abuse. Most of all, she came to a place of peace within herself.

A year later, I was having a coffee at a local café in Colaba, and the waitress turned out to be a former student at Don Bosco. She told me that forgiveness had restored harmony to her family. Her father was an alcoholic and sometimes beat her mother when he came home drunk. She and her mother had decided to forgive him instead of living with fear and anger. He was so moved by their forgiveness, the beatings stopped and he moderated his drinking. Forgiveness provides the power for reconciliation.

Practising the art of forgiveness

Because of life's ups and downs and the various relationships we cultivate throughout our lives, there is always something or someone to forgive. I find self-forgiveness to be the most challenging. When I catch myself regretting something I said or did, I know it's time to sit quietly and practise forgiveness with myself. After I acknowledge how I could have done better, I like to imagine how I would do it differently and how that might have changed various outcomes. I can't change the past, but I can imagine new futures from my present state of being. The best thing about mistakes is how much we learn and then we never have to repeat those mistakes.

The intention with forgiveness is simple and direct and will open you to consider the possibility of forgiveness in your life.

- Today, I am willing to forgive myself and others.
- In this way, I will give forth of myself with love and compassion.
- I am willing to forgive all that I have experienced as hurtful.
- I am willing to let go of the hurt so I can make a fresh start.

It is also helpful to write a forgiveness letter to both yourself and to anyone whom you have not forgiven. It is not necessary to send the letters—these letters are for you, for your own clearing and completion. You can also ask for forgiveness for anything you have done that was hurtful to someone. This process helps to clear your heart and mind so that you do not carry around any baggage. A big weight will be lifted, which will enable you to move forward with greater power and resilience.

Forgiveness is a practice that can be done daily to keep your inner slate clean and clear. In this way, nothing will obstruct your growth and your ability to extend love.

A forgiveness practice

Sit comfortably. Close your eyes and take a deep breath—inhale to the count of four, exhale more slowly to the count of six.

Think of someone (it could be yourself or someone else) that you have not forgiven. There is no need to judge yourself or that person—just let the thoughts and feelings come to the surface. Whatever arises with regard to this is presenting itself so that you can look at it with fresh eyes and accept it as a part of your history. In this acceptance, allow yourself to let go. Holding on will only hold you back. Letting go will free you to move forward with your life.

You are not forgiving a hurtful act, you are forgiving that person for forgetting their own goodness and for being incapable of loving. They forgot who they truly were and lost their regard for you. In remembering your own loving nature, you remember this person's loving essence beneath the surface.

When you are ready, bring that person's image to your mind and say quietly, 'I don't like what you did but I forgive you'. In your forgiveness you acknowledge their humanity as you send forgiveness to dissolve the impact of the negative action that hurt you. This is over now. It cannot hurt you anymore. Send it back into the past with gratitude for the learning it brought you. Allow your heart to be filled with peace. Allow this peace to radiate outward to fill your whole being.

Is there anyone from whom you need to ask forgiveness? Bring an image of that person forth right now in your mind. See them sitting in front of you. Simply say 'I ask your forgiveness'. Imagine your two hearts connecting. All is forgiven. Love has returned. There is only love. You and this person are now harmoniously complete.

When you are ready, slowly open your eyes and take another long, deep breath and then exhale slowly.

This can be done at the end of each day before you go to sleep to clear your heart and mind of negative thoughts and feelings left over from the day.

9

Patience

'Love is patient. Love is kind.'—1 Corinthians 13

Forgiveness is a process that takes time to assimilate. As we have explored in the last few chapters, forgiveness is an outcome of acceptance, listening, speaking the truth and coming to an understanding of our thoughts and feelings about a life event, whether large or small.

None of this can be rushed, and it's best that you take time to work through each part of the process. Patience is required. Patience creates the space for what is needed to transpire. This applies to most challenges that arise on a daily basis. Forgiveness may not always be necessary, but patience is almost always required because what we want to happen often has its own timeline.

I learnt a lot about putting patience into practice when I was in Mumbai. One particular day stands out.

Journal entry, 24 April 2015

Meeting K.P.—A Lesson in Patience
'The woods are lovely dark and deep . . . '

Finally, the meeting was set. It took three weeks of multiple phone calls and emails to set an appointment with the Additional Police Commissioner of S. Mumbai, Krishna Prakash. We were meeting him to present our programme plan for Emotional Intelligence Training, to be custom designed for S. Mumbai police. Our corporate programme trainers, Mohan and Shruti, were as eager as I for this meeting. The success of this programme would mean the beginning of groundbreaking work and many more programmes throughout the city that would serve to build trust in community/police relations. We showed up in the office waiting room twenty minutes before the appointed time. It was the usual hot, humid day in Mumbai, but the entrance was wide open and the ceiling fan was whirring overhead. A slight breeze took the edge off the sweltering heat.

To pass the time we googled Krishna Prakash (affectionately known as K.P.) and discovered an article online that said he had a habit of quoting poetry in meetings and speeches. One of his favourites was a poem by Robert Frost: 'The woods are lovely dark and deep but I have miles to go before I sleep . . . miles to go before I sleep.' I couldn't believe it—those were the very same lines I had on my Facebook profile page in the section 'About You'. I was bursting with excitement as I shared this with the group. 'Brilliant,' said Mohan, 'You've got to show him.' I quickly found the page in question on my smartphone to be ready for that moment. Not one, not two, not three . . . but four hours later the moment came at the end of a forty-five-minute meeting during which Mohan and Shruti communicated in

Hindi and Marathi how they would create and orchestrate a unique programme using dramatic skits to illustrate the common challenges faced by S. Mumbai police and how these were usually handled. The police officers attending could then give their feedback to suggest more positive ways of resolving these issues involving the use of emotional intelligence.

True to form, K.P. began quoting the poetry of Indian poet Tukaram in the local language, Marathi, looking straight at me, while Mohan and Shruti translated. It was something about a person who forged ahead in the midst of a dark storm and emerged victorious. Tears filled my eyes, and then I showed him the Facebook page on my phone, pointing out the lines from the Robert Frost poem. A big smile spread across his face as he said, 'Yes, we have miles and miles to go—and we will!'

Yes, we waited over four hours for our meeting with K.P. Though initially we were restless, we decided to surrender with acceptance and patience. During this time, we caught up on our phone calls and emails and got to know each other better. If we had not had all that time, we would never have discovered K.P.'s favourite poem. The fact that K.P. and I shared a love for Robert Frost formed a bond that engaged his full support for our programme. This led to a much more committed programme about five months later that culminated with a cricket match for peace between the expat businessmen cricket team and the Mumbai police cricket team. The police won the match by a landslide of course, but we created a day of fun, goodwill and friendship to build trust between the police and the community. This is a powerful example of how patience paid off in both the short and long term. Because we were patient, we even had fun while waiting.

Living in a state of peace requires patience. Patience is being kind to ourselves and to others. Patience is compassionate and loving. Patience is so many positive things that it is actually to our benefit to be patient. In the quiet space of being patient, peace is present. I learnt to trust in the timing of life. I've realized that I cannot control time, but I can choose to be patient as I watch everything unfold perfectly in its own time. And that becomes the perfect timing.

I learnt to slow down and enjoy life in a new way in the noisy, fast-paced city of Mumbai. Patience was one of the valuable gifts of my time in this unique and magical city, and for this I will always be grateful.

Practising the art of patience

I explored the art of being patient while taking care of my mother. Dying of cancer is a slow-motion death. Chemo and radiation treatments may or may not cure the cancer, and so there is a lot of waiting for results, waiting for signs of healing and the possibility of life continuing for a while longer.

Journal entry, June 2011

To be loving includes being patient. Patience allows things to unfold slowly and prevents negative energy from blocking progress. Today I will make this my focus. I discover I am patient sometimes but not all the time. I am impulsive and like to make things happen quickly. A lot of waiting is required these days. I settle in to waiting at the doctor's office and at the chemotherapy centre. Am I waiting for my mother to live or waiting for her to be healed? She is healing in her own way. I can see that she is becoming more peaceful during this process. She is determined not to die. She is patient and living day to day, hour by hour, accepting this routine.

A physical therapist comes over twice a week to help her build strength in her legs. They get along quite well, and I hear laughter coming from the bedroom where they are working on stretches and leg lifts. As she is leaving, the physical therapist tells me that my mother is her favourite patient. She said the rest of them complain but Mom laughs and giggles as she fumbles with the exercises. I love listening to the laughter—it's my favourite part of the day, so I make sure not to leave the house for a dip in the pool when the physical therapist is there. I am appreciating these little joys so much more than I ever have before. When life is on the edge, it feels so raw and intense. I notice I can't take anything for granted anymore. In the past I assumed that life would go on and on the way it always has. Now I wonder how I could have ever been so unaware and complacent. I felt peace from my daily meditations, but I was not fully engaged with life. I was somewhat detached and just let things flow by me. This is not possible anymore. I must be patient with life as it is. Life is certainly patient with me.

At the beginning of your day, you can read out loud or write down these statements of intention to increase patience:

- Today, I am willing to be patient.
- I accept things as they are with patience and understanding.
- I am patient with myself and others. There is no need to push or rush through the day.

- I will allow life to unfold in its own time.
- I am open to the experience of peace that patience brings into my life.

We learn best through direct experience. When challenged with impatience, this is an ideal opportunity to notice what triggers you. By bringing awareness to your challenges, you can move through them as you learn more about yourself and make a conscious choice to be patient with yourself and others. We are grateful when people are patient with us, so take a deep breath and be as patient as you can. Being patient is a loving gift for yourself and others.

10

Simplify

'Life is really simple but we insist on making it complicated.'—*Confucius*

There are many ways in which we complicate our lives. I discovered simplicity in my life as an outcome of slowing down, acceptance, listening, speaking the truth, forgiveness and patience. All these practices brought balance into my life and simplified my thoughts, emotions and actions.

We bring peace to our lives by simplifying. Less is more, and that includes less unnecessary talking, less running around helter-skelter, less clutter (both inner and outer). When life is less complicated, we are more balanced and peaceful. Life is dignified in its simplicity.

We complicate life when we resist it, when we judge it, when we want it to be other than it is. Stress is the result of resistance, clogging up our thoughts and emotions. This inhibits our capacity to be loving.

Journal entry, June 2011

Today my intention is to simplify. The first step will be to remove unnecessary clutter and distractions. In this way I can keep my life flowing smoothly without complications. I am willing to let go of what is not needed or what does not serve a purpose.

I discovered that life becomes simple when I do not resist what is happening. Once again, acceptance is required. Slow down, smile, breathe deeply, accept. This is not always simple, but it leads to simplification.

The challenge for me right now is finding beauty in simplicity. Yes, my life became simplified by circumstances that I did not choose. My mother's life has become both simple and more complicated by her lung cancer. She cannot do very much and has no need to go anywhere except for doctors' appointments and her chemo treatments. She brings a book to read while she's waiting. She doesn't feel the need to go anywhere else, she would rather be in her comfortable light-blue recliner reading or watching her favourite shows. She doesn't turn on the TV until later in the afternoon, so it's quiet in the house most of the day. I like the quiet. It's simpler than noise. To sit and do nothing is simplest of all. How rare that is, to do nothing and not feel that something has to be done or something is not getting done. To just sit in the simplicity of doing nothing is such a luxury. We don't call that meditation and yet that is the best meditation of all.

Yes, simply be. As Krishna said to Arjuna on the battlefield in the Bhagavad Gita (Chapter 2, verse 45), 'Be without the three *gunas*, O Arjuna, freed from duality, ever firm in purity, independent of possessions, possessed of the Self.'

The three gunas represent the field of relativity, constantly weaving together and interacting in the play of life. As humans, we are constantly in the midst of the craziness of life, but we can step back and take a view from the silence of being, the ultimate in simplicity. Pure being is pure awareness with no interference, no stories, no interpretations to confuse and complicate our thought process.

Our actions will then become empowered with this simplicity. Form follows intention. We fortify our intention by bringing our attention to our thoughts. From the foundation of a balanced state of mind, we can create the actions that will produce the most positive outcomes.

Can simplification work the other way around—from the outside in? Yes! Begin with the complications in your life. What is creating the most clutter, conflict, stress and stagnation?

Our lives become cluttered with old habits, relationships that no longer serve to enrich us, limiting beliefs that hold us back. Taking some time to reflect upon how your life is cluttered will reveal what can now be released. What are you willing to let go of? Acknowledge your current situation and all that it contains. What is no longer needed? Sometimes we accumulate things, store them away, and they end up taking up space in our closets. This happens with habits and beliefs as well. We follow the same routines every day because it's what we've always done. We don't question it. Now is the time to question your daily routines if you want to make a fresh start and open new avenues of growth, creativity, inspiration and abundant success. Let go, simplify, clear space, and new energy will come flooding into your life.

Begin with physical space—what can you throw out or give away? A common rule of thumb is to remove anything that has not been used in over a year. The simplest actions you can take are right in front of you. Devote a whole day to simplifying your physical space. Take a tour around your house and go through every room, every closet, every drawer in your desk, kitchen, bedroom. Create three piles—give away, throw away or recycle things that are no longer needed.

As you declutter and simplify your physical space, you will create an environment that is clean and beautiful in its simplicity. This will support the next step—to simplify your daily routine.

Slow down to simplify. Begin by directing your intention:

- Today, I will explore new ways to simplify my life.
- I create beautiful open space in all areas of my life as I simplify.
- I am willing to let go of negative thoughts that clutter my thinking and emotions.

What activities can you cut from your routine to simplify your day? What activities can you combine to save time and energy?

When your outer life is balanced, you will have more time for the quiet reflection necessary to experience the simplicity of being still. Resting in stillness, just being, is the simplest experience to have. Simplicity is peace. Peace is simple if we allow ourselves the time to slow down and experience whatever is happening in the present moment, just watching, listening, enjoying our own presence.

> In a simple moment
> nothing needs to be said,
> nothing needs to be done.
> In a simple moment
> I am alive.
> In a simple moment
> I am simply here.
> I am grateful
> For this simple moment.
> This moment just is.

Whether we experience complications or simplicity depends on where we choose to put our focus. We can create a harmonious day by beginning with balancing our body, mind and emotions. To balance the body, simplify your diet. Know what diet is most suitable for you and plan accordingly. To keep the body strong and healthy, exercise must be a part of your daily routine. This need not be complicated. Pick one or two ways to be active that are easy for you to add to your routine. For me, walking works best. It's complicated for me to join a gym or take classes. But I can always walk no matter where I am.

I have a friend who loves to dance, and she makes sure to just put on some music and dance every day in her own home. Another friend loves golf and finds plenty of fresh air and exercise in a four-hour game of golf at least twice a week. My oldest son Aaron has loved skateboarding since he was a young teenager. He's now thirty-seven years old and still takes the time to head over to the skate park for a couple of hours. My younger son Adam loves to walk and hike amidst nature. He and his wife have a dog who takes them out for a long walk twice a day. My eighty-three-year-old father still jogs twice a week. He has always loved running and is trim and healthy because of this lifelong habit. Doing what is easy and what you love is the simplest way to stay balanced and feel healthy.

How does forgiveness simplify life?

Forgiveness is the simplest way to maintain inner peace and unclutter your emotions. Forgiveness may not be a simple process and can take time, but once we have forgiven, we have let go of negative emotions that can clog up our hearts. Forgiveness simplifies our lives. Forgiveness allows us to set down another suitcase full of resentment. This brings more peace and helps you simplify your life and your emotions. It becomes one more reason to choose forgiveness as an act of self-love.

11

Have Fun

'The more fun you have, the greater your value to yourself and to your society. The more fun you share with others, the more fun you have.'—The Oaqui

'It's fun to have fun but you have to know how.'—Cat in the Hat by Dr Seuss

In the years after Alan and Naomi were killed, it felt like the fun had been sucked out of my life. Birthdays and holidays were challenging rather than happy occasions. It was during the time that I was caring for my mother when she was dying of lung cancer that I learnt a new lesson about having fun.

Journal entry, June 2011

Mom's hair has been falling out due to the chemo treatments. She decided to shave it all off this weekend right before her

4 p.m. happy hour. Auntie Ann and Lorrie came over to make it a 'shaving the head' party. Lorrie did the honours. Up in Atlanta, my brother Steve surprised us with a photo of himself with a shaved head. He decided to support Mom by shaving his own head at the same time. He is a bank manager, so it was quite a radical thing to do, but he wanted to do it to feel more connected to Mom during this time. Mom has a pretty face, and it looks good on her. She showed us that day how to turn something sad into a fun event. For dinner that night she just wanted an ice cream sundae. She said, 'We're in Florida, we can have whatever we want.'

After years of cold dreary winters in Michigan, Mom decided enough was enough. She made a conscious choice to live out the rest of her days in the sunshine state, having as much fun as possible, so she moved to Florida. After many months of living in Florida with my mother, I decided to make having fun more of a priority. I returned to Mumbai later that year with a renewed purpose added to the agenda of peace education—to have fun! Setting that intention made all the difference. One day I noticed an announcement in the *Times of India* that the Cat in the Hat would be appearing at a local bookshop. I had read the Dr Seuss books to each of my children numerous times until they could read for themselves. I couldn't miss a chance to meet the Cat in the Hat, so I hopped into a taxi and went to the bookstore. It was fun to see all the kids lined up to shake hands with the Cat in the Hat. I lined up along with them and had a photo taken. I couldn't help but laugh at myself, but it was a lot of fun. In fact, it was the first time I had had fun all by myself since Alan and Naomi had died.

Travel by car in Mumbai is slow due to the heavy traffic. When I looked out the window on many long trips across the city, more often than not, I would observe people having fun. I saw a lot of smiles and laughter, singing and dancing. Whether or not it was a holiday, it was common to see some kind of celebration on the streets of Mumbai.

It was the young students of Mumbai who surrounded me with an infectious joy of living. I had so much fun being with them; their enthusiasm was contagious. High school students from Don Bosco in Matunga were inspired to hold a peace rally to 'honour the sacredness of life'. They lit candles to honour each of those who had lost their lives in the 26/11 terrorist attack and sang a song of peace from the prayer of St Francis:

Lord, make me an instrument of your peace,
Where there is hatred, let me sow love;
Where there is injury, pardon;
Where there is doubt, faith;
Where there is despair, hope;
Where there is darkness, light;
Where there is sadness, joy.

I gave a short talk on forgiveness as a pathway to peace. It is also a pathway to joy, as I soon found out.

When it came time for questions, someone raised their hand and asked, 'How old was your daughter?' I told them she was thirteen years old and that she had had aspirations to be a heart surgeon so she could save lives. One of the peace rally organizers then announced, 'Let's have all the thirteen-year-olds come up on stage and surround

Madame Kia.' To my surprise, about twenty-five students rushed up to the stage and they said, 'We're your family now. You are not alone.' Tears streamed down my face as I was overwhelmed with gratitude for this compassionate gesture. These students showed me that I could feel sad and have fun at the same time.

The most unexpected fun I had in India was when I travelled to the Cheetah Camp slum on the outskirts of Mumbai to introduce an education project created by a group of students from St Andrew's College. The school where the classes would take place was deep inside the Cheetah Camp, so my cab driver Sameer insisted on parking the cab and escorting me to the school. It was the first time I had ever been inside a slum. It was a busy community bustling with activity.

As we walked towards the alley leading to the school, we came across a large dirt field where several boys were playing cricket. We stopped and watched the game for a few moments and then one of the boys called out, 'Do you want to play, ma'am?' I thought, well why not? They handed me a cricket bat that I held like a baseball bat, which gave them all a good laugh. I was soon shown the proper way to hold it and then managed to hit the ball on the third throw.

There was much jumping and cheering, and as I was running back and forth between the wickets, I noticed a dead rat lying on the pavement next to the field. I jumped back shouting, 'A dead rat!' The boys just laughed and said, 'Yes ma'am, no problem.' Apparently, a dead rat was not going to interfere with their cricket match, and so they carried on as if it were nothing. I took a deep breath and decided to ignore it. Sameer and I thanked them and eventually found our way to the school where over a hundred children of all ages were waiting.

They had given up their Sunday to take part in an afternoon programme to enhance their maths and English skills. Their faces beamed with eagerness, and I could see this was a special occasion for them. It was fun to watch their smiles as they listened intently to the college students explaining how useful it was to learn English and how it would provide greater job opportunities. They were so motivated and looked like they were enjoying every minute. I found myself enjoying every minute as well, just looking at those beautiful faces and feeling grateful to be sitting in the midst of a very different culture from my own. My daughter would have loved to be there too. In a way, it was she who had brought me there, and I felt close to her that day, knowing how much fun she would have had if she had been there.

I knew that Alan and Naomi would not have wanted me to spend the rest of my life feeling sad, but I had to allow the sadness to envelope me before I could say, okay, enough is enough. The sadness was my personal winter and India provided the sunshine that brought some joy back into my life.

Practising the art of having fun

This is not something we create by thought alone, but if you feel resistant to having fun, it helps to create a mindset that is open to fun for the sake of fun and nothing else. Once you set your intention, you will allow fun to enter your life in new ways. Fun leads to joy, a precious gift of life.

Tell yourself, 'Today, I am open to having fun in unexpected ways.' Sit quietly for a few moments, breathe deeply and let go of all judgements and resistance. Sometimes I smile at my resistance and refuse to let it take over my day. I allow it to be there, but I focus more on the experience I choose to have. Today is a day to have fun in simple ways, so that is where I will put my attention. I will embrace this focus with love, gratitude and a smile.

Reflections: Here are some reflections to ponder as you open your heart to having fun in new ways. Write down all the possible ways to have fun and allow for a few surprises as well. Remember that you can create fun out of almost anything as you let go of old patterns and discover new fun and new joy.

How can you create new ways of having fun today?

When did you take yourself too seriously?

Were you able to let it go and have fun anyway?

12

Honouring Agreements

'Your life works to the degree you keep your agreements.'
—Werner Erhard

There are many agreements we make in life on a daily basis.
For example, I made an agreement with myself with
regard to taking care of my mother:

> My agreement right now is to do my best to make life
> easier for Mom while she is going through her cancer
> treatment. Silently I have agreed to keep things simple,
> to give her privacy and space so that she can keep to her
> routine as she chooses without unnecessary interference.

To keep peace and harmony flowing in life, it is important
to honour our agreements. I try to do what I say I'm going
to do, be on time, and be fully present. To honour an
agreement we have made with ourselves or with others is

a choice. It is a choice to be respectful and to live with integrity. To dishonour an agreement brings negative responses and negative outcomes. Is this what you would choose? When you honour an agreement, you are living with honesty and authenticity. When you honour your agreements, life remains balanced and whole.

There are times when we have agreed to do something or be somewhere at a certain time but are unable to do so due to circumstances beyond our control. Life is often beyond our control, but we can navigate the fluctuations.

Some effective ways to create mutually beneficial agreements with others are:

- Communicate honestly to create understanding so you can come to an agreement.
- Forgive self and others and/or ask for forgiveness so you can move forward.
- Explore alternatives that would work to fulfil what is required so that you both benefit.

In this way, harmony is maintained in your relationships and balance is restored.

What if we want to change our agreements? Are there agreements you have made that are no longer relevant or appropriate? Choosing to live with integrity and respect for life is choosing to honour your agreements, so you need to know what your agreements are and if they are in line with your authentic self.

Notice your resistance to various agreements. What are you struggling to follow through with? Resistance is a signal that something needs readjusting. It is either your attitude or you need to renegotiate to change your agreement. Determine what you can do easily and do that. Break it up into smaller parts. Accomplishing a piece of your task will pave the way for completion.

A classic example of an agreement with oneself is the story of Gautama Buddha sitting under the Bodhi tree. After seeing the suffering of humanity, he pledged to himself he would sit under the Bodhi tree until he reached the ultimate state of enlightenment—a state of awareness beyond suffering. Only then would he re-engage with the world. As the story goes, it took seven weeks of sitting non-stop for him to reach this state. He then devoted his life to teaching others.

A friend shared a modern example of a life-changing agreement with himself. He sold his company in England and decided to start a new chapter of his life in India, where he had previously done some business. He made an agreement with himself that he would live in India for one whole year, no matter what happened. He rose to the challenge and ended up staying for ten years. He left because he had made an agreement with himself that he would return to England in 2017 to the city where his ninety-one-year-old father was in his final years. In following through on both these agreements, he brought forth new experiences, new challenges, new joys and new friendships.

For him, this was his way of sitting under the Bodhi tree. By making these choices, he aligned himself with his true nature and remained true to himself. Buddha did what was true for him at that time in a completely different context, but in both cases, awareness of self was achieved. Buddha withdrew from outer life and sat still until he experienced pure being and thus transcended his individuality. My friend embraced life to the fullest extent possible and found a larger version of himself in the process.

Before you can even begin to honour an agreement it is important to know what outcome you wish to have and if this agreement is appropriate for you. Ask the important questions first:

- What is expected of you?
- Is there a deadline and does this timing work for you?
- Is this agreement in harmony with your other agreements?
- Will there be a conflict of interest or time?

Listen to your heart and ask if you can be fully committed to this agreement before you agree. Once you have agreed, have faith in your ability to deliver what you agree to do. Give it your best. Keep your focus and do not allow distractions. Communicate honestly when delays or challenges arise. If something is not working, it is important to say so and adjust the timing or other details so that you can remain in alignment with your agreement. Take your agreement seriously by embracing it with love and respect.

Make a list of every agreement you currently have. Begin with agreements you have made with yourself:

- Diet
- Exercise
- Self-development
- Spiritual practice

What agreements have you made with others?

- Work
- Family
- Friends
- Romantic relationships

Are all these agreements still valid? Are there any agreements you need to renegotiate?

Evaluate each agreement to determine its current relevance in your life.

What have you learnt about yourself through these agreements? What no longer works? What new agreements are most appropriate for this time in your life?

This is another way to simplify your life and create space for growth and transformation.

What is the most important agreement you can make with life? I think it must be an agreement to love life, love yourself and love your fellow human beings. If we agree to love one another, all else will fall into place.

When I learnt the Golden Rule in my younger years, I decided I would do my best to abide by it: 'Love your neighbour as yourself'.

It is also stated as, 'Do unto others as you would have them do unto you'.

Almost every religion has some form of this rule for life, which is a way to live with love for oneself and others.

- Treat others as you would want to be treated.
- Listen to others as you would want them to listen to you.

- Accept others as you would want to be accepted.
- Speak the truth to others as you would want them to speak the truth to you.
- Forgive others as you would want to be forgiven.
- Be patient with others as you would want them to be patient with you.
- Honour your agreements with others as you would want them to honour their agreements with you.
- Respect others as you would want to be respected.
- Love others as you would want to be loved.

This is a simple way to be the most loving human being you can possibly be.

13

Sharing

'Thousands of candles can be lit from a single candle, and the life of the candle will not be shortened. Happiness never decreases by being shared.'—Buddha

In the course of our lives, we share a variety of things. We share what we have, what we know and who we are. We share our time and attention—or not. Sharing is a choice. We don't have to share, but life tends to flow more easily when we do. Most of us are taught by our parents and teachers that sharing is good. We were taught to share our toys, our food and whatever else we had when someone was in need. It's not always easy for children to share, especially with brothers and sisters. As adults, we are especially choosy about sharing—who we will share with, what we will share, when we will share and how we will share. We can withhold or give to whatever extent we choose. We can choose to share love or withhold love. We can share of ourselves or withhold our thoughts and feelings from others. To give forth or hold back, that is our choice in any moment of every day.

Sharing creates connection with life and the people in our world. Withholding cuts off connection, resulting in distance and separation. Sharing increases the flow of love and connection to one other. Increasing love is a gift we give to ourselves as well as to others in whatever form it takes.

An experience of sharing friendship

Meeting Mrs S. became my most significant new friendship after getting to know the Sachdevas, a family that provided friendship and assistance to my husband when he was coordinating the Mumbai retreat for our group of meditators. One day, in Mumbai, as I was sitting in Gautam Sachdeva's office drinking tea, he called an elderly friend, Mr S., who was the president of a Mumbai club and suggested we all meet for lunch. Gautam told me that this man and his wife had lost their son and daughter-in-law in the terrorist attack at the Tiffin restaurant at the Oberoi hotel. They were there at the same time as Alan and Naomi. It was their favourite restaurant and they ate there often.

The Cricket Club was nearby, so we were soon sitting in the restaurant with Mr S. who told us his wife would be joining us shortly. Several minutes into exchanging pleasant conversation, Mrs S. arrived. We all stood up to greet her as she approached the table. She walked slowly and gracefully towards us. She was wearing a beautiful silk saree. She was about my height (about 5 feet 2 inches), and as we extended our hands, our eyes met. No words were spoken, we just stood silently for several seconds and then each of us nodded in a silent greeting. No words could be spoken between us as we joined hearts, knowing that each had lost a child in a terrorist attack just two years ago.

This was one of the most intimate first meetings I have ever experienced. I could barely eat lunch, so I listened to the conversation. Mr S. is a warm-hearted extrovert, adept at keeping the conversation light and friendly. Mrs S. was composed and quiet, but at some point, she turned to me and asked if I would like to accompany her to her house in Alibag that weekend. I didn't know where Alibag was, so I looked over to Gautam who was nodding encouragingly. 'Sure, I'd love to, thank you,' I said. She then told me she would have her secretary call with details.

A few days later, I met gracious Mrs S. and a few other guests of hers near the entrance to the ferry boat pier at the Gateway of India, from where we were to take a boat for the one-hour ride to Alibag. The other guests were young lawyers who were working with Mrs S. on a special litigation project regarding the 26/11 attacks. They all spoke in Hindi and Gujarati, so I never got the details. I was told they also worked to reveal corruption and file charges when scams were uncovered.

When we docked at Alibag, we were met by their drivers, who took our bags and delivered us to the beautiful estate. It was a lush tropical property right on the beach, with its own pool. There were stone Buddha statues at the entrance, and as we walked into the front room, a large

framed quotation that covered most of the wall caught my
attention. My eyes filled with tears by the second line.

> 'Death is nothing at all. It does not count. I have only
> slipped away into the next room. Nothing has happened.
> Everything remains exactly as it was. I am I, and you
> are you, and the old life that we lived so fondly together
> is untouched, unchanged. Whatever we were to each other,
> that we are still. Call me by the old familiar name. Speak
> of me in the easy way which you always used. Put no
> difference into your tone. Wear no forced air of solemnity
> or sorrow. Laugh as we always laughed at the little jokes
> that we enjoyed together. Play, smile, think of me, pray for
> me. Let my name be ever the household word that it always
> was. Let it be spoken without an effort, without the ghost
> of a shadow upon it. Life means all that it ever meant. It
> is the same as it ever was. There is absolute and unbroken
> continuity. Why should I be out of mind because I am out of
> sight? I am but waiting for you, for an interval, somewhere
> very near, just round the corner. All is well. Nothing is
> hurt; nothing is lost. One brief moment and all will be as
> it was before. How we shall laugh at the trouble of parting
> when we meet again!'—Henry Scott Holland, St Paul's
> Cathedral, 1910

How beautiful, I thought, for Mr and Mrs S. to embrace
this perspective and share it with every guest who entered
their home. We still hadn't shared anything about our
losses on that day, but I was slowly being introduced to
this remarkable family. There were framed family photos
all over the main reception room and several photo albums

I was encouraged to view. The young couple had left behind two teenage daughters who the grandparents were now raising. 'We can't break down, we have to look after them,' Mr S. said. I rarely saw the girls in person but got to know their family life through the many photo albums that captured every birthday, vacation, holiday and anniversary. Love, happiness and the celebration of life shone through every one of those photos.

Mrs S. lived up the road from the hotel where I was staying, and she invited me to have lunch with her every day, sending her driver to collect me and drop me back. We got to know each other gradually, even though we often ate in silence. It felt so comforting just to be with her. One day as I was leaving, she took my hand and said, 'You don't have to be alone.' I will be forever grateful for her generous heart and the warm friendship that she shared so graciously.

The most important thing we all share is life itself. I have come to realize the importance of prioritizing the value of this life more than ever. Loss provides a deeper appreciation of that which was lost. The experience of our shared humanity hit home after the Mumbai terrorist attack. It is the most powerful sharing of all, and I know if I can fully embrace it, I will always be at peace.

Practising the art of sharing

Once you set your intention to sharing, this focus will bring opportunities to share as well as noticing the sharing that is going on around you.

You can open to the gift of sharing with these intentions:

- Today, I am open to the experience of sharing.
- I am sharing who I am from my heart.
- I share with love, kindness and compassion.
- I am honouring the sacredness of life by sharing the truth of who I am.
- I joyfully share my experience of life with everyone I meet.
- I am grateful to find new ways of sharing and look forward to this experience.

Share whatever is most appropriate at the time, either alone or with others. My friend Gautam shared his friends from the club and, in turn, Mrs S. shared her home, her friendship and her support each time I visited Mumbai.

Journal entry, June 2011

I realize that my mother is sharing an intimate gift with me. She is allowing me to be here with her as her life either continues in good health after her chemo treatments or comes to completion and she does not survive. She is sharing her sweet home and whatever this time brings to us as we carry on with daily tasks and doctors' appointments. Sharing life with another person is the most precious gift. I haven't lived with my mother since I was seventeen years old. In my high school years, I was intent on ignoring my parents as much as possible. I spent most of my time in my room with headphones on listening to my record albums. And now Mom is sharing an experience she doesn't want to be having but yet here it is, this cancer that might be cured through these treatments that caused her hair to fall out. She is tired all the time, she does not have much of an appetite and when she does eat, she cannot always hold it down. She still says, 'I'm not ready to die'. She is willing to go through all of this so she can live longer, as long as possible, even with the oxygen machine and the walker now required to help her get from room to room. I know it annoys her, but she accepts it. She doesn't believe she is going to die from this cancer, and I admire her optimism. I feel privileged to be here. I don't think she realizes she is sharing anything special, but I feel I am the recipient of something rare.

Reflections: The following questions will help to give you insights into your experience of sharing (or not sharing). Reflections on these questions will show you how you limit your sharing and once acknowledged, can open you to a deeper experience of sharing in your life.

Was there anything you did not want to share and chose to withhold?

What is being shared with you by the people around you?

Were you a miser in any way?

Did you share something new?

How did you share and how did it affect your experience?

Did you share communication or withhold communication?

14

Receiving

'For every beauty there is an eye somewhere to see it. For every truth there is an ear somewhere to hear it. For every love there is a heart somewhere to receive it.'—Ivan Panin

Receiving the experience of life is infinite. The gifts we receive from life come in many forms. When you open yourself up to sharing, you are also opening yourself to the other end of the spectrum—receiving. How open are you to receiving what life is offering in this moment?

I found that forgiveness provides an opening to receive more of the positive experiences of life—joy, inner peace, love, laughter, celebration, serenity and creative inspiration. This is why forgiveness is a gift we give to ourselves. Not forgiving is holding on to that which hurt us, angered us or traumatized us. We then become a hostage to that experience and remain a victim of negative impact. Forgiveness will free you from those bonds and you will eventually move beyond surviving to thriving.

Here is a beautiful example of receiving the magical experience of India while on a walk in Mumbai. I came across a letter my husband Alan had written to friends while he was in Mumbai in June 2008. He was exploring the options for the best venue to hold a spiritual retreat with a group of people from the Synchronicity meditation group. His writing clearly shows how much joy he was experiencing in India, and when I read this my heart swelled with love. I had the pleasure of visiting that exact spot in Mumbai many times in the years after the attacks.

Gateway of India

Welcome, dear friends. I greet you from India where I find myself once again at Master Charles' request. I am here in Mumbai (Bombay), India's most populous (and perhaps popular) of cities where cultures, languages and aspirations mingle in what could be the ultimate melting pot. Given the daily temperatures even in this, the monsoon season, melting pot is as literal a term as it is metaphorical.

My purpose in spending two weeks here is to prepare the way for Master Charles' tour scheduled for November 2008 with twenty-five participants in this unique spiritual retreat. On a daily basis, I interact with our Indian partners, who are long-term Synchronicity Associates who have a very successful spiritual book publishing firm, which also serves as the distributor for Synchronicity products in India. Likewise, I maintain daily contact with Master Charles via email, updating him on various aspects of this endeavour as it unfolds. There must be something of India in my own soular history as I find that even though it is a foreign, and in many ways, strange culture, I feel very much at home and at ease within it. It is as if I know it on a subtle level and can very easily navigate its idiosyncrasies . . . and almost everything in India is idiosyncratic!

The place (where) I am staying is very near the ocean . . . a five-minute walk and I am strolling by the sea along a road that runs parallel to it and which is enjoyed by many as a promenade. Any time of day or night, there are people walking along the sea wall, just for the pleasure of Being. Some of Mumbai's most familiar landmarks are also here next to the sea . . . the world-famous Taj Hotel and the Gateway of India, an arched monument of concrete that is reminiscent of the Arc de Triomphe in Paris.

As we are in the midst of the monsoon season, torrential downpours may last for many hours or even days. At times, the rain is so overwhelming that trains must shut down and many businesses close due to their employees being unable to make it to work. The ocean takes on a very different character in these times and becomes very turbulent. While walking I watch in awe as the waves rise high and break against the sea wall, cascading over the edge and splashing loudly on to the sidewalk. Pedestrians have to remain very wakeful lest they become soaked.

To add to all the excitement, thousands of pigeons gather on the plaza adjacent to the Gateway of India. One moment they are covering the ground, pecking away as onlookers toss them handfuls of grain or crumbs. All of a sudden, they take to the air as a noisy unified diversity and the sky is filled with their beating wings and cries, while the sea churns and tosses its waves.

Cars and taxis are scurrying past, horns blowing constantly . . . as is the Indian way. An occasional dog struts by. A street urchin comes towards me, begging for a few rupees. A man with giant balloons to sell tries to entice me. A young man asks me if I smoke grass and would I like to buy some. A mother and her two young children are sitting down on the wet road eating scraps of food they have foraged from the garbage. Two men are sleeping soundly on the sidewalk. The smell of frying food, spices and rotting waste fills the air. A wealthy Sikh man in a beautiful turban leads his family from a Mercedes to the front entrance of the Taj. Two young German women walking by in revealing tops and thigh-high shorts draw bewildered stares from the local Indians.

I turn the corner and the wind is gusting in my face. The rain is starting up again and I open my umbrella and keep walking . . . I feel blissful and free . . .

As you can see, when Alan felt happy and free while walking in the monsoon rain, he was receiving Mumbai's gift of life. He would have missed it if he had cursed the rain. Instead, he embraced it fully as he walked through the diverse crowds across from the Taj Hotel at the Gateway of India. In his openness, he allowed the grace of receiving to enter his grateful heart, one of the many gifts he received from India in his final days. In my last conversation on the phone with him, he said, 'I love India so much I could die here.' I know he meant that in the most positive way, so it is ironic that India is indeed where he took his last breath. I hate how he died, but there is some comfort in knowing he was in a place he loved so dearly.

The letter from Alan encompasses what he received from India. Naomi received many gifts including silk scarves and ankle bracelets, but her prize gift was the nose piercing. For months she had been begging for a nose piercing. She was only thirteen and although ear piercing was common in America from a young age, nose piercing was not. We finally gave in to her request on her trip to India, and she enrolled the assistance of the Oberoi hotel concierge to find a reputable piercing specialist to come to the hotel. On my last phone call with her, which took place a few days before the terrorist attack, she was so excited to tell me about her nose piercing. She sent a beautiful photo that showed the delicate gold stud in just the right place. She looked so elegant and grown up I was happy she finally got her wish.

One of the things I received on more than one occasion in Mumbai was surprise encounters. I was invited to give a talk on forgiveness as a path to peace at a bookshop in Bandra, a suburb of Mumbai. After the talk a man came up to me and said, 'I knew your daughter. I used to be the Oberoi hotel concierge. I helped her find the best person to pierce her nose and arranged for him to come to the hotel.' I couldn't believe it! But there it was—we hugged and had a photo taken. I left with a heart full of joy. I felt more and more that Mumbai was like home, and I was surrounded by family. This was a precious gift I received again and again.

Practising the art of receiving

If you want to receive, put yourself in a receptive attitude by creating an intention for receiving.

- Today, I am open to new ways of receiving.
- I am open to receiving wisdom, insights, guidance.
- I am open to receiving smiles, hugs and friendship.
- I am open to receiving love.
- I am open to receiving creative inspiration.

These are examples of some experiences I like to receive—make your own list of everything you received today and don't hold back. You may learn something about yourself in the process. If you are open to embracing and allowing yourself to receive what life is offering, you will discover hidden treasures buried underneath the surface, waiting to be found.

15

The Gift of Gratitude

'As each day comes to us refreshed and anew, so does my gratitude renew itself daily. The breaking of the sun over the horizon is my grateful heart dawning upon a blessed world.'—Terri Guillemets

Inherent in sharing and receiving is gratitude. Every single day there is some form of sharing and receiving. Sometimes we are grateful to the people in our world, sometimes they are grateful to us. Gratitude is often present but not always expressed. Gratitude is more than just a 'thank you', it is also an acknowledgement of and appreciation for a person, place or experience that is happening in our lives. It could be a warm breeze, a ray of sunlight breaking through the clouds, birds singing or an act of kindness—nearly everything can be an opportunity to be grateful. People and things come and go as life flows on. We breathe through it all—we are alive to experience life with all the negative and positive experiences it brings. Life itself is certainly something to be grateful for.

There is much we take for granted; it is easy to be cynical about the benefits of gratitude. There are certainly some things in life we are not grateful for, so there is no need to pretend. At least once we know we don't like something, we don't have to choose it again. I once had coffee with a friend in a small café by the sea. We thought it would be charming and serve delicious coffee, but it was not to be. It was crap coffee, and the café was noisy with bright lights. My friend's comment took me by surprise—instead of complaining about it, he said, 'I'm so pleased we came here. Now we know never to come again.' Instead of resenting our choice, he managed to be grateful. He wasn't trying, it just came out that way and then we could laugh about it instead of moaning and groaning about a wasted trip. We had a brisk walk by the windy sea and found another café that served strong, freshly ground coffee. We appreciated that coffee even more and were grateful for the unexpected find.

Once we choose to focus on the positive aspect of any experience, we will find something to be grateful for. Why is it so important to focus on gratitude? Gratitude is another form of love. Gratitude connects us to love. If we turn our attention to gratitude, there will be infinite opportunities to be grateful. Giving and receiving gratitude feels wonderful. It costs nothing and gives so much in return. In this way we give and receive love all day long. Love is an enjoyable, fulfilling experience we give to ourselves, and gratitude is one way to keep the flow of love alive.

I discovered the value of intentional focus on gratitude with a group of young people from Delhi on Christmas

Day in 2013. After Avnit Kaur, a university student from Meerut, attended a talk I gave on holistic education at Ramanujan College at the University of Delhi, she expressed a desire to practise my thirty-day peace pledge with her family. We exchanged emails during this process, and she was so happy with the results she wanted to do more and was inspired to create a peace project in Delhi with her friends. She said there were always 'terror alerts' in the city so why not create a 'peace alert' and surprise people with spontaneous acts of positive peace. She organized a group of about ten friends to practise a peace flash dance and visit Central Park in Connaught Place in Delhi to dance, sing and collect messages of gratitude from strangers. People were delighted to share their messages of gratitude and join the peace dance. They were asked, 'What are you most grateful for?' and wrote their message on a blackboard to be photographed and posted on Facebook. We had conversations about gratitude with dozens of people on Christmas Day, each one eager to share. We learnt that most of the things they wrote down had to do with family or friends. They were most grateful for 'mom and dad' or 'my brother or sister' or 'my best friend'. It was all about relationships. All about love shared. Love is what most people are grateful for.

Hidden treasure

Dip into the well of gratitude and you will find an infinite spring of love.

Gratitude is the hidden treasure within any experience, even a sad one, such as the loss of a family member or close friend. Within the pain of the loss is the love and appreciation we felt for our dear one, as well as the memories of the happy times we shared with them. Within gratitude, it is possible to experience both sadness and love, the pain of loss and the joy of the memories. There can be laughter amidst the tears as we remember fun and funny incidents. When I think of Alan and Naomi, I am grateful for every moment I spent with them. I am equally grateful when others share their memories of Alan and Naomi with me. I often learn something new about them, something else to cherish, another hidden treasure.

Journal entry, July 2011, Ellenton, Florida

I know my mother is grateful to be alive, so grateful that even after a bout of throwing up in the bathroom after a chemo treatment, she came out saying, 'I feel so blessed.' I couldn't believe she could feel blessed in that moment, but it caused me to realize that she felt blessed to be alive enough and strong enough to make it to the bathroom and heave her heart out. I feel blessed to be here. I feel blessed to feel love and appreciation for these sacred moments. I feel blessed to have shared my life with Alan and Naomi for those years we had together. I am grateful for the opportunity to share more love with the world. I know I will be returning to Mumbai later this year. My mother will either be stronger and won't need my help in the same way as she does now or . . . she won't be here anymore. A sad thought. But I am grateful she is well enough to get up and down, use the walker, laugh at the Cash Cab *TV show, drink her wine, eat ice cream and do her crossword puzzles in the morning.*

Practising the art of gratitude

To take on gratitude as a practice is beneficial for the body, mind and spirit. It provides a positive outlook on life that can coexist with the negative experiences, bringing with it a return to a balanced state of being.

To intentionally practise gratitude, you can begin with statements of intention, such as: Today, I am open to giving and receiving gratitude. I am open to experiencing gratitude in all areas of my life. I allow my resistance to melt into the river of gratitude.

There are also some actions you can take to strengthen gratitude. A lovely way to begin and end each day is with a prayer of gratitude. A grateful heart needs no words, so such prayers may be silent communion.

Express appreciation and acknowledgment whenever possible. Just say 'thank you' and share why you are grateful.

Write a thank you letter to yourself—what do you love and appreciate about yourself?

Write a thank you letter to a close friend or family member. Whether you choose to send it or not doesn't matter. Just write down what you love and appreciate about them. What are you grateful for in this relationship? Even negative relationships provide valuable lessons, however painful.

To whom and for what else in your world can you express gratitude? Are there any other messages you can send—to local leaders, teachers, service providers—that express your appreciation for the part they play in your world?

I wrote this tribute after my spiritual teacher, Master Charles Cannon, passed away to express my love and gratitude for the many years of inspiration from his wisdom and guidance.

The guiding light

There is a light in my life that never dims, a light that has increased its brilliance over the years as I made my way through dark tunnels, smoke and mirrors, thunderstorms, thick grey clouds and the downpouring of a thousand tears.

When the biggest thunderbolt of all split my life into shatters, instantaneously blasting away so-called reality, the quiet steady voice of Master Charles opened me to the possibility of a greater vision. It was Master Charles who suggested we create a positive outcome to the tragedy of the Mumbai terror attack. It was Master Charles who had to step over the blood, debris and dead bodies at the Oberoi hotel and identify Alan and Naomi. When I could not bear to return to my home, it was Master Charles who said, 'Your home is here, you can stay here forever.'

It was Master Charles who gently, patiently kept me under his wing, providing all that was needed during a never-ending healing process. It was Master Charles who nurtured and encouraged the spreading of my own wings so that our message could be shared all over the world.

This was the blessing, the gift of love and compassion in response to an act of terror. The light of Master Charles is the light of love and compassion. It is a miraculous light that continues to grow stronger as I open myself to receive it. Master Charles adeptly showed us all how to open our hearts and minds and stay open so that this light surrounds

us, moves through us, protects and shares its wisdom
through each of us.

Master Charles' entry into my meditative life was a
major turning point that led to more and more turning
points. I learnt to integrate love into every moment of my
day. I learnt about the mechanics of balance, which gave
me the tools to play the game of life more effectively. These
tools proved to save my life later on when tragedy struck.
Not only did the guidance of Master Charles save my life,
his spiritual presence alone kept me from falling over the
edge countless times over the past twenty-five years since I
first arrived at Synchronicity.

The empowering light of my teacher is the light that
shines forever, dispelling the darkness. The light of Master
Charles ignited the light that destroyed my illusions,
freeing me to be all that I can possibly be.

Why was he called 'Master' Charles? This designation
was given to him by a grateful student who felt such benefit
from his transformational teachings that she addressed him
as Master Charles. He showed us how to master being
human by being balanced and whole. It wasn't meant as
'master over other people' but rather master chef, or master
musician. He was a master of the art of meditation and
holistic living.

16

Celebration

'Each day holds a surprise. But only if we expect it can we see, hear, or feel it when it comes to us. Let's not be afraid to receive each day's surprise, whether it comes to us as sorrow or as joy It will open a new place in our hearts, a place where we can welcome new friends and celebrate more fully our shared humanity.'—Henri Nouwen

Every celebration is an expression of love. Celebration brings joy, laughter and the blessings of family and friendship.

After honouring the second anniversary of the 26/11 attack, a group of us travelled to Varanasi, the ancient city of Shiva on the sacred Ganges River. Mark Twain said of Varanasi, 'Benares is older than history, older than tradition, older even than legend, and looks twice as old as all of them put together.'

Because we were with our spiritual teacher who had studied in Ganeshpuri for twelve years and was an ordained Vedic monk, we had the privilege of staying at an ashram for Brahmin priests in training. The head guru was a ninety-eight-year-old swami who was revered by everyone in Varanasi. Each afternoon a brown and white cow walked through the gates into the ashram and went straight to the guru's room to sit at his feet for an hour or two. I watched this in awe, knowing that this was another of those things that happened only in India.

When we arrived on this sacred ground, I felt peace for the first time that year, like a sweet, warm blanket was enveloping me as soon as we got off the plane. I was floating for the next five days. It was hardly quiet, but there is a distinct stillness beneath the noise, especially in Varanasi. All day and night, there were drums beating and people chanting as processions marched down the narrow alleys with bodies on stretchers on the way to the burning ghats. The bodies of the deceased were wrapped in bright yellow, gold or silver fabric strewn with flowers. Cows, goats, monkeys and dogs mingled with the processions as they made their way along the lane to the ghat for the cremation of the bodies. Kites flew overhead all day, dotting the bright blue sky with colour.

Being in Varanasi was like stepping back in time. It was older than anywhere else I have ever been. I had heard many stories about the Ganges River. Everyone in our group decided to take a dip at sunrise to receive the blessings from the river. The idea horrified me. I had heard that the river was full of urban sewage, animal waste, pesticides, fertilizers, industrial metals and rivulets of ashes from cremated bodies. However, Sanjay, our guide, said that the water was divine, and if we dipped into it as divine water we would be blessed, and no harm would come to us. I knew my husband would have jumped at the opportunity and would have been the first to take the plunge. I wanted to honour Alan by taking the dip in his place, knowing he would be there in spirit. It was early morning as we quietly made our way to the bank of the river. The sun was just beginning to rise in the distance. Varanasi was slowly waking up and we could smell incense and chai among a unique combination of smells.

We bought some flowers to offer the river as our guide chanted prayers. As I looked up at the rising sun I thought of Alan and said, 'This is for you, Alan.' I then took a deep breath and dunked my head under the water. Sanjay said, 'Three times, you have to dip three times.' We were all fully dressed as is the custom and were soaked to the bone. We walked back to our rooms, dripping along the way, laughing and feeling happy. Washing up felt so good I didn't even mind the cold water from the bucket that was my shower. Technically I was covered with polluted water that Indian doctors warn people to avoid bathing in, but I felt cleansed and purified.

The famous Shiva temple was one of the sites that was highly recommended, so we went for the evening aarti. It was full of people pushed up against each other and pushing forward to reach the Shiva lingam to toss their flower offerings. I thought I was moving forward, but so many people were pushing ahead of me I hadn't made any progress. I realized I would have to push forward with more aggression, otherwise I would remain where

I was. I inched forward with people pushing behind me and I pushed in front of me, and somehow we all moved together. I managed to toss the flowers in the air, hoping they would land in the right place. And then all the lights went out. Apparently, this happens often in Varanasi. It was pitch black. We were barefoot and had to feel our way back to the entrance. I stepped on something squishy and realized it was a pile of excrement. I quickly eliminated it being human because that would be too dishonourable in a temple. Cows were too large to get into this spot, but monkeys were around, so I determined it had to be monkey shit. 'Only in India!' I thought, and all I could do was laugh. What a day—I had begun with a divine dip in a river full of it and had now completed this crazy day by stepping in a pile of shit. One thing I learnt to count on in India was the unexpected. I learnt to let go of how I thought things should be. What did I know anyway? Not much. As the days went by, the more I let go of what I thought I knew, the liberated I felt.

With an open heart I returned to Mumbai and felt ready to make a fresh start and celebrate a new year. A friend of mine shared that he had eaten lunch with one of his friends at the Tiffin restaurant at the Oberoi, where Alan and Naomi were killed, and drank a toast to Alan and Naomi. I loved that gesture and decided to do the same on New Year's Day 2011.

I had been in the lobby of the Oberoi hotel a few times but so far had been unable to bring myself to enter the restaurant. I knew it was time to stand in the very place where Alan and Naomi had been shot. To fully accept their deaths, I had to see where it had all happened and embrace their spirits in that spot. I needed to enter the heart of this darkness to find my way back to a new life.

I felt so vulnerable and shaky as I approached Fenix from the passageway connecting to the Trident where I was staying. It was in between normal mealtimes, so the restaurant was fairly empty. I walked over to the back corner where I had been told Alan and Naomi had been sitting that night. The restaurant had been completely renovated by this time—pure white marble replaced black marble, and of course, all the tables and chairs were new as well. I stood not knowing what to do, but a staff person came over and said, 'I know who you are. I was there that night. You look like your daughter. They were sitting right over here.' He then pointed to the very spot. He said he remembered everyone at the table laughing and enjoying themselves. I told him that Naomi had ordered her favourite meal at the Tiffin—asparagus sushi—that night. He said, 'Yes, we still make it, do you want some?' I nodded and then sat down at a small table nearby.

He brought me some magazines to look at, and I ordered a glass of champagne to drink a silent toast to the new year. I didn't feel like eating anything, but I felt Alan and Naomi's presence strongly. It felt like they were encouraging me to toast the new year with an open heart. I honoured their request as best I could. I didn't feel alone at all. I felt sad, but I was also genuinely looking forward to a new life, a life that would include them within my heart. This was indeed something to celebrate.

Celebration is an outcome of gratitude. Sometimes we celebrate a completion; sometimes we celebrate the launch of a new project. I have come to enjoy simple things to celebrate in the course of a day. It may be silly, but it is a small way of enjoying ordinary life. I can't take anything for granted anymore. I'm surprised by how much I did take for granted before. I know too well how quickly life can change, so I now appreciate each moment more than ever before. When it feels challenging to celebrate, I find it helpful to spend time in places where other people are celebrating. I think that is why being in Mumbai was so healing for me. People in India are always celebrating something. I know this is why I was drawn back there again and again for many years.

Celebrating as a practice

There is no need to wait for a birthday or a holiday to celebrate. There are many creative ways to celebrate each day. It is fun to create celebration as an intention for the day and then see what unfolds. Being open and willing to celebrate in new ways will attract new experiences to celebrate. These intentions will set the stage for celebration as you read them to yourself or say them out loud.

- Today, I am open to celebrating ordinary moments throughout the day.
- I celebrate the vibrant life that is happening all around me.
- I celebrate the beauty that fills this world with joy.

Reflections: To dive more deeply into the experience of celebration, reflect on these questions and write from your heart what comes to you as an honest response.

Can you open yourself to celebrating your life just as it is right now?

How did you find yourself challenged or resistant to celebrating?

What did you experience when you opened yourself to celebrating ordinary moments of the day?

17

Inclusion

'We need to give each other the space to grow, to be ourselves, to exercise our diversity. We need to give each other space so that we may both give and receive such beautiful things as ideas, openness, dignity, joy, healing and inclusion.'—Max de Pree

What does inclusion have to do with forgiveness and why is it important?

Forgiveness enabled me to include a negative, painful experience but at the same time release the negative emotions over time so that I was free from the impact. I did not want to be stuck in grief, loneliness and moral outrage for the rest of my life. I chose to become more loving in my attitudes, especially towards people who held different beliefs with regard to politics and religion. I gained a deeper respect for a variety of perspectives and learnt more about each subject in the process.

Each of us views life from a lens uniquely coloured by our past experiences, how we were raised, and what we were taught. This lens is valid for each of us. It shapes who we are and how we feel, think and react to life experiences.

If I am willing to acknowledge that your lens for viewing the world is different yet just as valid as mine, I include you. I can't see through your lens, only you can do that. You can share your experience with me, and I will learn from it. If I exclude you, I miss out on that view. Including you expands and enriches my world. I learn more from you than I would on my own or through reading books. If I exclude you, I miss out on many opportunities—to hear stories about your life, to share with you stories about mine, to enjoy your company, to laugh with you, cry with you, share a hug or a sunset dinner, eat an ice cream cone or celebrate a holiday. Your holidays may be different from mine and may come at different times of the year. Including you means including your holidays and increases the opportunities to celebrate in new ways.

If I exclude you, I maintain a narrow view of the world. I limit my capacity to experience a kaleidoscope of colour reflected in the diversity of life experiences we share with each other.

If I include you, I acknowledge your value as a human being. If I exclude you, I disregard your worth. Every one of us is worthy and has something of value to offer this world just by virtue of our very existence. Even if we don't have much in common, your presence in this world matters. I include you when I acknowledge this. Inclusion is a loving attitude towards life. Love is inclusive. Love embraces all differences. We all exist in the inner circle of life. We all deserve respect for our existence.

What I have learnt about inclusion

Life includes a spectrum of opposites. My meditation teacher Maharishi Mahesh Yogi taught us that 'the whole is more than the collection of parts'. The whole includes the parts, and these parts are diverse. Later in my spiritual life, my teacher Master Charles Cannon taught us that, 'In the great play of consciousness, everyone appropriately plays their part. Everything is as it should be—because it is.'

To wish that something were other than it is creates a struggle with life. Life contains opposites and everything in between, some of which we prefer and some of which we do not prefer. This is natural, but it is helpful to recognize that life is all-inclusive. We can include an experience as part of the reality of our lives and yet still choose to participate or not. I choose not to participate in hatred and revenge in response to terrorism. Instead, I choose to practise forgiveness, which has offered a bridge back to love. Love is wholeness, focused on the whole rather than individual parts. We can include the parts and then choose what relationship we will have with those parts.

My mother had no choice but to include cancer in her life. Inclusion is acceptance but also more than that. Sometimes we exclude people who are different from us, but we can't always exclude circumstances that we don't like. To include is to live with it rather than push against it. To resist causes us to be miserable if we can't change it. To include is to accept the reality of a situation and do what we can to learn from it, change it, or make the best of it. We're working on changing my mother's cancer cells to healthy cells. We include the reality of what is happening but we also do something about it to create the best possible outcome.

Reflections: These reflections will help you to gain insight about your ability to include and what patterns or experiences of exclusion you may have had in your life.

Are there ways you could be more inclusive?

What or who have you excluded in your life? Why?

Have you ever been excluded? How did that feel?

Can you include different points of view even if you don't agree?

Can you communicate your opinions respectfully?

It is important to stand in our own truth, but it is also important to respect someone else's truth even when we don't agree. We can walk away and choose not to engage, but we can include the difference as part of the vast tapestry of life.

If you want to expand your heart by becoming more inclusive, you can strengthen your focus with these intentions:

- I am open to expanding inclusion in my life.
- I am willing to include experiences as they happen and then respond.
- I include everyone in my world with love and respect.
- I include my choices as learning opportunities.

18

Flow

'Flow with whatever may happen and let your mind be free. Stay centred by accepting whatever you are doing. This is the ultimate.'— Zhuangzi

Flowing with forgiveness makes it possible for life to flow freely without obstruction. Unforgiveness is like having a clogged drain where water cannot flow. Unforgiveness clogs up emotional energy, which backs up on us and becomes toxic. To keep this energy clear and flowing, it is necessary to choose forgiveness. This is worth giving your full consideration, knowing that you are the one who will either benefit or suffer. You may have already suffered from an event that hurt you deeply, but there is no need to keep suffering. It's over now, the past is over. The past is not the present. Forgiveness allows you to renew yourself and thus renew your life. The power to forgive is in your heart. This is the choice—to use it or not to use it. To forgive or not to forgive. To forgive will be giving love back to yourself, love that was denied, dishonoured, rejected or abandoned because of something that occurred involving someone you knew, possibly loved, or someone who was a stranger. It doesn't matter, that part of it—just know that you hold the power to love or not to love. Someone else may have lost their capacity to love, but you do not have to join them in a loveless state. You can choose love by choosing forgiveness.

When you forgive you will flow with life rather than against it. Flowing with life brings harmony and peace. Flowing against life brings struggle and stress.

As I was going through my daughter Naomi's sketchbook one day, I found a simple drawing of butterfly wings with the words 'Flow Love' written underneath. Flowing love is just as soft and gentle as the fluttering of butterfly wings. I noticed my heart was flowing with gratitude in that moment, for the beautiful reminder from my daughter. She is still here in so many ways.

Flowing gratitude is indeed flowing love. How else can you flow love today?

I find that setting my mind to flow and bringing my attention to the flow of my breath is an easy way to relax into a peaceful flow to begin the day. Our thoughts direct our experience, and this is a good thought to set the tone for a harmonious, flowing day.

To allow my day to flow more easily, I wrote this prayer:

May this day be blessed with the natural flow of life, and may I meet it fully without reserve.
May love flow through my heart, mind and actions, bringing harmony to this day.

May water flow where it is needed on this earth.

May fresh air flow among the trees and cleanse our cities with fresh oxygen.

May sunlight flow into our gardens, our farms, our lives.

May love flow from my heart into the hearts of others.

May love flow into my heart and fill my being with peace.

May I flow with the current of life as it carries me forward.

May my words flow with truth, wisdom, love and respect.

19

Kindness

'You cannot do a kindness too soon, for you never know how soon it will be too late.'—Ralph Waldo Emerson

·

Kindness is an act of love. Acts of kindness take many forms—a simple smile, patience, listening, speaking the truth with respect, a willingness to understand, expressing gratitude, doing someone a favour without expecting anything in return, sharing time, resources or knowledge to help a family member, friend or even a stranger.

I remember being helped by a stranger when I found myself almost out of gas on a dark, cold night in rural Virginia. Alan, baby Naomi and I were in the process of moving to Virginia and we drove in separate cars to our new location. I had Naomi and our two cats, Topsy and Fluffy, with me in our Toyota Corolla. I had mistakenly packed my wallet with cash and credit card in the moving truck, which Alan was driving. As it was getting dark,

I missed the exit to the small town where we were renting a cottage in the Blue Ridge mountains. About an hour later, I noticed the car was running out of gas. Desperate measures were called for, so I pulled up to the first house I could find with lights on. Holding Naomi in my arms, I knocked on the front door, hoping for kindness. A man answered and looked a bit suspicious at first, but when I told him the situation, he invited me into his home, where his family had just sat down to a large dinner. They insisted I join them and only after they had served me a large slice of homemade apple pie and fresh coffee did they ask how they could help. I told them I needed to use their phone to call my husband and borrow some money for gas. Alan had been frantic wondering where we were. Once he heard what had happened, he explained how to return to the right exit. The man insisted on following me to the nearest gas station to make sure I didn't run out of gas on my way there. I borrowed $5 and took his address, assuring him I would send cash back to him. He said it wasn't necessary, he was happy to help. In a time when most people distrust strangers, I felt taken care of and welcomed in a time of great challenge and was so grateful for this kindness.

Kindness connects us to each other as it allows for a flow of goodwill among fellow human beings. Kindness doesn't ask for anything in return, it simply extends love. Kindness expands our beings, bringing forth an opportunity to express our true nature, which is naturally loving and compassionate.

Kindness to self

Kindness is most often extended to others and less often to ourselves. Beginning the day by being kind to ourselves is a good start to a day. What that looks like would be different for each of us.

What would being kind to yourself look like? What are the types of kindness you like to give and receive?

There are both small and big acts of kindness. I like small kindnesses because they are more frequent and add up to quite a treasure chest of wonderful experiences. Sometimes a big kindness takes an effort, even though that effort is worth it just for the giving of it.

Kindness flows from an open heart as a natural expression of love. Putting love into practice includes kindness in the multiple forms it can take in the course of a day, often in the midst of the most ordinary experiences. While standing in line at the grocery store, I have often witnessed someone letting the person behind them who has just one item go in front of them. I have been on both ends of this situation. Even if we are holding one item and someone ahead of us has a full basket and chooses not to let us move ahead, we can take a deep breath and practise patience as we slow down and flow with a long wait. Either way, we win— we can practise kindness with ourselves by not giving in to frustration and impatience. In this way, we continue to be loving one way or another.

Practising the art of kindness

Remember that whatever we put our attention on grows stronger in our lives. Once we set our intention on kindness, we will see acts of kindness all around us. We will also attract opportunities to be kind. In addition, we can choose to do a random act of kindness that someone does not expect. This is great fun and creates surprising results that add to the enjoyment of life.

If we put our attention on the opposite of kindness—disrespect, selfishness, greed, harsh words spoken to another, we tend to see more of this behaviour around us. We attract the energy we put out.

There is an old story from the Native American tradition that illustrates this very clearly.

A little boy approached his grandfather one day seeking his advice. 'Grandfather, I am so upset and don't know what to do. I just found out that my best friend has betrayed me. I love my friend, but I am so angry.' The boy's grandfather said, 'I know just how you feel. There are two wolves who live inside of me. One wolf is peaceful, loving, kind, compassionate and forgiving, always seeking harmony. The other wolf is angry, full of hatred and feelings of revenge and wants to cause harm. These two wolves sometimes fight each other.' The little boy's eyes opened wide and he said, 'Grandfather, which wolf wins the fight?' His grandfather smiled and said, 'The one that I feed.'

Forgiveness is a kindness we give to ourselves if we feed the 'good wolf' inside of us.

Opening to kindness

I use this simple blessing prayer I wrote for myself to set my inner compass to kindness.

May I be kind in as many ways as I can throughout this day.

May I be kind to myself as well as to others.

May I be open to unexpected acts of kindness. I respect the dignity of life in myself and others by being kind in words and actions.

May I be open to receiving kindness from others.

May this day be blessed with kindness in all ways.

Reflections: To deepen your experience of kindness, here are some reflections to consider so that you may gain insight into your experience of kindness at the beginning or end of the day.

What are some new ways you can practise kindness today?

Were there any times you did not feel like being kind?

Were you able to be kind anyway?

How did it feel being kind?

How did it feel when others were kind to you?

20

Collaboration

'Alone we can do so little. Together we can do so much.'—Helen Keller

Collaboration is all about connecting, communicating, coordinating and cooperating. In a state of balance, the heart and mind collaborate, creating a powerful partnership of inspiration, wisdom and creativity, combined with love and compassion. Forgiveness paves the way for true collaboration with life because without it we cut off the flow of love within ourselves. If we choose to collaborate with love, we must choose forgiveness. Love is the most giving collaborator. If we turn towards love it will guide us through broken relationships, loss, grief and loneliness.

We begin by collaborating with ourselves and that starts with the mind. The mind directs our attention through our thoughts. Collaboration with the mind is meeting our thoughts as they are and then directing our focus to what is required in the present moment. With a clear, focused mind we can make the most appropriate choices and take the best actions to fulfil what is needed. If nothing is needed, we can just enjoy the present without expectation or restraint.

An unexpected collaboration

Once I opened to collaboration, I was blessed with unexpected opportunities to collaborate in this unique and fun new way.

Because I stayed at the Trident in Nariman Point whenever I was in Mumbai, I had the opportunity to meet businesspeople from India and other countries, particularly the UK. I was invited to attend a British Business Group meeting that met monthly at the Trident. I met the president of the India Business Group, Vikash Mittersain, at that meeting and became an honorary member thanks to him. I also became an official member of the British Business Group so that I could learn more about how business could play a role in creating a peaceful society. I was surprised and delighted to learn that the game of cricket could play a role as well. At the time, I was conducting a peace alert programme with the Mumbai police to build trust in the community. When British businessman Matt Greenwell heard about the initiative, he said we should collaborate on a plan for a cricket match between the police and expat businessmen. He was part of an expat cricket team and thought they would all love the opportunity to challenge the police to a cricket match. We called it Cricket Match for Peace.

The intention was to create a collaboration to build police–community trust and get to know each other better in the process. After months of planning, the match was a resounding success. The police won the 20–20 match by a landslide but everyone received a medal, a celebration lunch and a *Pocketbook of Peace*—the English version for the expats and the Marathi version for the police. Not only that, one of our British team members had met the famous cricket guru Harsha Bhogle and invited him to come early to the match to pose for a photograph with the teams. Harsha graciously agreed and also accepted a *Pocketbook of Peace*, which he posted on his Twitter and Facebook accounts. This unlikely collaboration between an American woman, British businessmen, the Mumbai police and a well-known cricket commentator resulted in thousands of people in India and many other countries becoming inspired by a message of peace. We all want peace in our daily lives as well as in our world. Peace is more than the absence of war. Peace is a collaborative joining of hearts and minds in harmony with our shared humanity. We are at peace when we are having fun. This cricket match was a stunning example of having fun, celebrating the game of cricket in a unique way as we brought together diverse players from different races, religions and cultures.

Practising the art of collaboration

Create your statements of intention to bring focus to collaboration. In this way new collaborations will find you!

- Today, I am willing to collaborate in new ways, beginning with myself, bringing collaboration between my heart and mind.
- I extend my collaboration to everyone I meet.
- I enrich my experience by collaborating with life itself. I am open to the experience life brings to me on this day.
- I collaborate with love, respect and gratitude.

Here are some reflections to deepen your appreciation for the benefits of collaboration.

Were you able to turn conflicts into collaboration?

Were you able to find new ways to collaborate with yourself and others?

How did you collaborate with yourself today? How did you collaborate with others?

What did you learn about yourself in this process of collaboration?

21

Inspiration

'For my part I know nothing with any certainty, but the sight of the stars makes me dream.'—Vincent Van Gogh

Inspiration fuels my motivation to take action. Inspiration comes from both my heart and mind. Inspiration helps me create something new. To be inspired and to share inspiration is to feel more alive from the core of my being.

Journal entry, July 2011, Ellenton, Florida

Here on the Gulf Coast of Florida, we have the ocean to inspire us. The ocean makes me feel alive and full of inspiration. My sister and I offered to take Mom to the closest beach, about a half hour away for a short day-trip if she was feeling up to it. She said yes, she'd love to hear the ocean but felt she may not have the strength after her chemo session to walk from the car to the beach. But she was willing to take the trip, so off we went.

It was a beautiful warm sunny day with a slight breeze, a perfect day for the beach. We found a spot where we could set up our chairs near the car to minimize walking for Mom. The water was just over the sand dunes, and we could hear the waves but could not see them. We knew it would be too arduous for Mom to attempt walking over the dunes, so we relaxed in our chairs, happily soaking up the salty air and sunshine. There was a food stall nearby, so I walked over to get us some ice cream. Simple pleasures become the sweetest experiences at such times. Mom's strength was waning, and although we didn't talk about it, we knew she might not last through the summer. I think she cooperated with this beach trip to please us because she was happy to pack up and head home. She is more inspired by her blue recliner these days than anything outside the house. In the blue chair she can simply rest and just be, without having to do anything else. She doesn't want or need to do anything else. She is content and at peace. I feel inspired and humbled by this simplicity.

Life provides infinite inspiration each day—from sunrise to sunset, life is renewed each day. Every day we have the opportunity to make a fresh start if we are open to the inspiration that is right in front of us, within our very own hearts and minds. Inspiration touches our souls, opening us to a larger version of ourselves. Inspiration gives us the inner strength to weather the storms of life. Inspiration is looking towards a greater vision of our current reality. It can lift us from darkness into light in the form of art, music, poetry, stories, nature, acts of kindness and compassion. Life is renewed by inspiration. Inspiration motivates us to extend ourselves with love in whatever way is unique to us. Love itself is the most inspiring. Love inspires us to reach out and connect with others, lend a helping hand or express what is in our hearts and minds.

I remember being inspired by the story of Siddhartha, who became the Buddha. I wanted to experience the same inner peace he had attained through meditation. This led to learning transcendental meditation. I was so inspired by my experience of inner peace that I became trained to teach Transcendental Meditation so that others could also experience this peace. Peace is here in the present moment, we just have to allow ourselves to relax and let go.

'Inspiration comes from a quiet mind.'—Master Charles Cannon

When our mind is quiet, we are not disturbed by our thoughts. When our mind is quiet, we experience the present moment in its totality. We become aware of our feelings, senses, perceptions and insights. A quiet mind enables us to listen from within and to feel what arises from the source of our being. Life itself becomes an inspiration when we slow down to allow the fullness of life to envelop us. Life is then renewed from within. When we connect with the depths of our own being, we open the window of creative expression.

Before Alan and Naomi were killed in the terrorist attack, I never thought of life itself as inspiring. And certainly not immediately after the attack. I learnt that life can be taken away at the snap of a bullet and what remains is forever changed. I was left with myself and myself alone most of the time.

In the stillness of this aloneness, something stirred as I sat watching the wind blowing through the leafless trees. It was the time of year when all the leaves had died, but the tree danced in the wind, looking beautiful, graceful and at peace with itself. The season was changing, but nature was very much alive. My life was changing, and I was still breathing, my heart was still beating; I felt both heartbroken and full of love at the same time. I wanted to stay connected to life and learn to love life as a new me. I felt inspired to create a positive outcome of some kind in some way, shape or form. How to do this, I had no idea, but I was inspired to find out.

Inspiration in the quiet moments of an ordinary day kept me moving forward. Those dancing trees reminded me to find my own dance as I let the winds of life surge through my being.

Generating inspiration from within

To become inspired from within, we must take an inward journey. Sit comfortably, close your eyes, take a deep breath and let go. Imagine diving into the ocean beneath the waves, into the stillness. Just be. When you notice thoughts crossing your mind, return your attention to your breath. You can use the following statements to open yourself to the experience of inspiration from within. Using words to set your intention will set the experience in motion.

Today, I am inspired by the experience of life that is happening moment to moment.

I am inspired by life itself. I inspire myself and others with love and respect.

I am open to new inspiration in the ordinary moments of my day.

Inspiration can take many forms and I embrace them all with enthusiasm.

I will carry this focus with me throughout the day with love and gratitude.

In addition to these statements of intention, there are some practical ways to find inspiration:

- Take a walk in nature—in the forest or by the sea or across a large field.
- Sit in a flower garden and notice the colours and scents, shapes and sounds.
- Visit an art museum and slowly walk around, taking your time to fully experience paintings or sculptures you feel drawn to.
- Listen to your favourite music while not doing anything else—just listen to each note.

These reflections will deepen your understanding of inspiration and how it plays out in your life

What inspires you most about yourself?

Was there a moment in your life that inspired a change in direction, a major decision or creative expression?

Have you ever experienced the extraordinary within the ordinary? In what way did this reveal itself?

Inspiration connects us to a greater vision and a higher version of ourselves. We honour this connection by acting on our inspirations.

22

Connections

'Humankind has not woven the web of life. We are but one thread within it. Whatever we do to the web we do to ourselves. All things bound together. All things connect.'—Chief Seattle

Human beings are part of a magnificent fabric of life, connected in one way or another. The extent to which we are connected to the source of our own being is the extent to which we can connect with others.

In truth, it is not possible to be disconnected, but we often feel isolated, cut off. Feeling disconnected is a misperception in our minds. Connection is where we extend who we are into the field of interaction. This is the becoming of being, the flowing of life into diverse patterns and unique expressions. We reconnect when we recognize that which is always present, the underlying consciousness that pervades all reality. This has been described in many ways and given many names, but in essence it is the divinity of life.

Connection with self

This is the first and most important connection. To connect with self is to know ourselves fully from the source of our being. Tuning in to the source is an inward journey done in silence. Connecting is bringing our attention to the presence beneath the thoughts and feelings. Once we choose to make that connection, we find it is already there. We only lose it sometimes when our attention is elsewhere, or our experience is overpowered by our thoughts and feelings.

To nurture connection with self strengthens it and provides a foundation for inner stability. To be grounded in this presence, knowing it is who we are on the soul level, is the most effective way to weather the storms of life.

When the biggest storm of my life came crashing in, I had been living at a holistic meditation sanctuary for eleven years. We lived a reclusive life as a family and followed the daily meditation schedule along with service in various roles over the years.

After the unexpected deaths in my family, part of me felt disconnected for a period of time. Ironically, I found my connection to life once again in the very place where they died—Mumbai. Not only did I become connected to their deaths in a personal way, but I was also blessed with many new connections that led to a life I could never have planned or even imagined.

The many years spent living in a holistic retreat established a deep connection to the inner self. There were minimal distractions from the outside world. The only distractions were those arising from our own minds, the stories we tell ourselves over and over that keep us bound to old identities until we are willing to release them as part of who we are, but not all of who we are. I learnt there is so much more to life than what appears on the surface. There is an unbounded ocean inside of me. As Walt Whitman so aptly put it, 'I contain multitudes'. In Mumbai I had abundant opportunity to connect with the multitude aspects of myself as well as meet the most diverse groups of people I had ever encountered.

I was introduced to educators, students, businesspeople, government leaders, religious leaders, police chiefs and Bollywood stars. As one connection led to another, I wondered what would come of it all. A wise woman named Ruby who ran a charitable trust said, 'It may not make sense right now so just keep meeting people, share your story and then over time you'll see how it all fits together.'

Steve Jobs, the creator of Apple, said it perfectly at his commencement address at Stanford University in 2005.

> You can't connect the dots looking forward; you can only connect them looking backward. So you have to trust that the dots will somehow connect in your future. You have to trust in something—your gut, destiny, life, karma, whatever. This approach has never let me down, and it has made all the difference in my life.

As I look back over the past twelve years, I have seen how my own dots have connected and have opened up a new world that led to the nourishing support I needed for healing and surviving a traumatic experience. I am grateful for each connection I was blessed to make in India. I learnt something valuable from each of them. Some of them have stayed with me and some have moved on, but none of them are forgotten. All of them have contributed something of value to my life.

Past connections—moving forward

It's over—the past is over now. It's over, but connections to the past do not have to bind us to the past. The remains can serve as a reminder of memories, of growth, learning and gratitude for the life in which they were contained. We move forward by acknowledging the value of past connections and what we learnt from them. Some of them will remain with us if they become friends or share our values and purpose in life. Some will join us to create a business or a community project, or to partner in an event with a shared purpose. Some will move forward on their own paths, and we can simply bless them with love and gratitude.

I am creating a new pathway from a new home in a new context that fits perfectly with who I am now. I am free to choose—free to celebrate, enjoy and love as I live in the service of bringing peace, love and compassion into the world, beginning with myself.

Connecting with others

'What you put your attention on grows stronger in your life.'—Maharishi Mahesh Yogi

This is a simple yet profound teaching that has stuck with me from the early years of my spiritual journey. It seems so obvious and yet how often I've allowed myself to be swept up in fear-based thoughts and feelings about people and situations. My ability to connect with others is based on my attention to either their strengths or their weaknesses, the light that shines out of their eyes or the clouds they carry from their own negative thoughts and feelings. We connect with that aspect of a person to which we put our attention. If I want to create a positive outcome—success, peace, harmony, love—I bring my focus to the outcome I wish to achieve and then who I need to be in relation to it so that I can do my part to create that outcome. There is much we cannot control, but we can control how we think, how we speak and how we act. I have found time and time again that when I respond with love, patience, harmony, forgiveness and understanding, I receive the same or more from the other person, even if there is a disagreement.

'Be the experience you choose to have.'—Master Charles Cannon

If I want to experience love, I must be loving. If I want to experience peace, I must bring peace into my world. In this way, I nurture my connections and attract new connections, new friends and colleagues with whom I can share inspiration and collaboration. Everything is connected and every day we are connected in a multitude of ways. We strengthen those connections with our attention and love. We can minimize or dissolve negative connections that do not serve us in a positive way. If we must interact with a negative person, we can bring forth the opposite to balance out the negativity. We don't have to respond in the same way. We don't need to connect with negative words and actions by being negative ourselves. We can be compassionate or at least be neutral. We can choose to distance ourselves. This is often challenging. Each encounter we have with someone presents us with the opportunity to learn and grow.

Practising the art of connection

To strengthen connection begin your day by tuning into yourself. How are you feeling? What thoughts are you having? Take at least a few minutes to sit quietly and connect with yourself.

Create the opening to new connections with these affirmative statements to set your inner compass.

- I am open to connecting to deeper parts of myself, to my whole self in all my dimensions.
- I am open to deepening my connections with friends and family.
- I am open to making new connections to enrich my life in new ways.
- I am willing to let go of connections that no longer serve my best interests.

• I am creating space for connecting with life in a more expansive way.

If you prefer to tune into yourself another way you can journal your dreams, or write your intentions for the day and what outcomes you would like to create.

Consider these reflections to gain insight about connections you may not have noticed before and new connections you would like to create.

As you go about your day, notice how you connect to those around you. Are there any new connections you want to make?

Are there connections you want to strengthen? How can you do that?

What did you notice challenged you about connections in general?

What did you learn about yourself and others as you focused on your connections and how you are connecting?

Is there anything you want to change or adjust?

We are connected to the whole of life. When we honour each of our connections with love and respect, we bring forth harmony and peace. It is a contribution we can make every day, a contribution that enriches the world with love.

23

Completion

'When we are motivated by goals that have deep meaning, by dreams that need completion, by pure love that needs expressing, then we truly live.'—Greg Anderson

Forgiveness brings a sense of emotional completion. We then have a choice as to whether to continue to complete a relationship. As we complete we let go of emotional baggage that can weigh us down and obstruct our growth and success. Completion takes time and so does forgiveness. Life is one long continuum, but within it there are many completions. We finish school, and even during our school years we complete exams, grades and eventually graduate. We complete some friendships while others will continue in our lives. Completions are a part of life and something to be celebrated. Completions clear the space for new experiences and new people in our lives. It helps to be aware of these completions so that we can fully learn from them and enjoy their passing.

The death of a loved one contains many completions. It is also the end of life as we knew it: the completion of a life lived that is now over, our relationship with the person who died, roles that are no longer needed or are no longer appropriate to the new situation, daily routines are completely overturned, and holidays that will never be the same. In fact, nothing will ever be the same. It takes time to adjust to this change. Life feels different. You feel different. In that process, we interact in a new and different way with family and old friends.

In essence, it marks the completion of a chapter in our lives. We are left to pick up the remains and 'move forward'. A few months after my husband and daughter were killed in the 26/11 terrorist attack, I was told by a well-meaning friend, 'It's time to move on'. I couldn't get my head around this, much less my heart. Move on to what? I felt incomplete on so many levels. I hadn't cried nearly enough tears. I needed to practise compassion for myself. I needed to learn how to love myself. My roles as wife of Alan and mother to Naomi were now complete. I had to practise acceptance of this reality. I was still in shock and it would take years to uncover and feel the depth of such traumatic and violent loss.

On a spiritual level, I knew that Alan and Naomi were two bright lights that would shine forever in my heart. My love for them would never die, and they would not be forgotten. Even though I was inspired to share a message of forgiveness, love, compassion and peace, I also needed to grieve this human loss of precious life. I needed to grieve the loss of my former roles before I could embrace a new life, new roles and new love.

Completions are important so that we can create new ways of being and open up new aspects of our lives. Incompletions clog up our lives and prevent us from moving forward.

Big completions take time and cannot be rushed. Big completions involve both mental perspectives and emotions. I found that I needed to become actively engaged in the grieving process in order to move with a completely different flow of my life.

To complete emotionally is to experience what has happened or is happening as fully as possible. It is also important to give expression to these strong emotions in some form—whether sharing with a trusted friend or family member, writing in a journal or through the creation of art or music—whatever works best for you is most appropriate.

If emotions are pushed down, it will have an adverse effect on our bodies, creating stress that could even result in illness or substance abuse.

I invite you to take some time to apply what we have explored thus far—slow down, smile or cry, breathe deeply, accept, listen and speak truthfully—to gain an understanding of your own process in this situation of death.

Death of a loved one is a major change on every level of our being. At the heart of it, it is a loss, and grief is the natural human response. Major change gives rise to the possibility of life transformation if we open ourselves fully to the experience without resistance. Completion is a gift we give to ourselves.

Completing with the past paves the way to a new future beginning right now. Otherwise, we carry the past with us wherever we go. A friend of mine compared this to carrying suitcases from past journeys. Once she started putting her suitcases down, one by one, she began to feel lighter and happier as she found herself smiling more often. She even started painting for the first time in her life, which inspired her to create her own art studio in her home. She is now able to express her creative self in brand new ways with this new-found freedom from the past. Completions will open new worlds in surprising ways.

Practising completion

You can use these statements of intention to focus your attention on completion. It is helpful to read these aloud and then add your own individual intentions.

* Today, I am completing what I have begun.
* In my completions I create balance, harmony and fulfilment.
* In my communications I complete responsibly with love and compassion.
* As I complete with the past, I open myself to new possibilities for happiness and success.
* I am complete within myself as I am. I am a whole and complete human being in love with life.

Here are some reflections to help you identify your incompletions. Once you clarify what your incompletions are, you can create a focus to complete and then move forward.

What unfinished business do you have left hanging?

What is your most challenging incompletion and how will you shift it?

What did it feel like to complete something today?

Do you feel complete within yourself?

Major completions take time and patience, so it's best to begin with small tasks and work your way towards bigger completions such as relationships and past history.

Completion is a way of honouring a piece of the life you have lived with love and gratitude for the learning it brought you. We learn something about ourselves from each and every experience. Choosing conscious completion is choosing to manage your life responsibly. Peace is the outcome. Completion is a gift of inner peace.

24

Creating Balance

'Life at its best is a creative synthesis of opposites in fruitful harmony.'—Martin Luther King Jr.

What do we mean by 'balance' and why is it so important? To experience the 'fruitful harmony' of 'life at its best' we must begin with ourselves. We provide the seeds for this fruitful harmony through our thoughts, words and actions.

It's easy to tell if we're out of balance because something feels off, we just don't feel smooth, and life doesn't flow. When we are out of balance, we are either ill or there is a feeling of stress inside. This keeps us from thinking clearly and having the energy needed to get things done and make the best choices. The best choices are those that nurture us and expand our appreciation of life, choices that support good health and well-being for ourselves and the world around us. The best choices bring us joy.

Forgiveness is a choice that will help restore balance to our hearts and minds because it enables us to let go of negative thoughts and feelings that can lead to stress and possibly illness. Forgiveness will not change the event or situation that caused us to feel hurt or angry or even outraged, but it can restore a sense of calm to our inner being. It can settle agitation and tension when we finally let go of the need for revenge.

Forgiveness will bring peace. Peace is a state of balance. This is the foundation of resilient living. Forgiveness is a step towards building resilience.

Creating a balanced life requires daily attention to the well-being of our mind, body and emotions. When these aspects are in harmony, our inner life blossoms into a state of serenity and love. To create this beautiful state of being depends on choices we make moment to moment, day by day. These are choices regarding diet, exercise, how we spend our time, with whom we spend our time, how much time we spend working, having fun, or in quiet reflection to relax and just be. We can create the flow of our daily lives with simple choices that result in various outcomes. What outcome do you want? It's up to you.

Imbalance has become acceptable because we know it so well. If imbalance is the normal everyday experience, then how do we recognize it and how do we shift it?

If there is no joy, something is out of balance. If there is no peace, something is out of balance. If there is no love, something is way out of balance. The playing field of life is a field of opposites, sometimes dancing together in perfect harmony, other times smashing into each other, creating disruption, stress, frustration, inconvenience or illness.

Mental balance involves bringing awareness to our thoughts and directing the mind towards positive outcomes through intention. We cannot control our thoughts, but we can use our minds to direct our thoughts. Focus on the experiences you choose to have rather than react to experiences beyond your control.

Practice for creating balance

Begin the day by writing down experiences you would like to have—not a 'to do' list but a list of how you would like to be and what results you would like to see manifested on this day.

What experience do you need to strengthen in order to bring more balance into your life? Do you wish to be peaceful? Loving? Harmonious? Truthful? Strong? Confident? Write each experience you would like to have and practise 'being' this experience by focusing your attention on this experience. Listen to your heart and let your heart guide you to the most appropriate focus for the day.

By first creating a positive mindset you will set your inner compass to direct the manifestation of that experience in a natural way without effort. With an inner compass set to joy for example, you will flow into interactions that bring joy, or remember times you were genuinely joyful. If joy seems too much of a stretch, try just relaxing into peace. A peaceful state of mind will be a quiet state of joy.

Mental reactions come in the form of the stories we create to explain or blame our circumstances. There will always be something we can latch on to in this regard.

The key is to balance the mind so that we may increase our clarity of thinking and ability to observe our thoughts.

When we become aware of negative thoughts, we can shift our experience without judgement, simply refocusing on the opposite as an alternative rather than cursing our current reality. Yes, we accept whatever reality is happening but then grab the reigns of the mind and determine what would work to adjust the situation to create a balanced outcome.

You can use your mind to guide your thoughts. For example, if I am looking forward to doing something with a friend and they cancel the plan at the last minute, I feel disappointed and could feel hurt and rejected or abandoned, but if I take some time to slow down, reflect upon the situation, I shift from the story of rejection to simply feeling the hurt inside myself. I accept it and allow the feelings to surface with understanding and compassion. If I allow my thoughts to dominate, I will remain stuck in the story of rejection. If I drop into my heart, I open up space for understanding and acceptance. I then let go with forgiveness as an act of self-love. Otherwise, I would carry resentment for my friend and would put up barriers to our relationship. I choose to let go of resentment and continue to feel loving. In this way I maintain harmony and inner peace.

Beware of judgement. Judgement creates conflict, division, separation and resentment. The remedy for judgement is a willingness to understand, acceptance, forgiveness and compassion.

Emotional balance requires patience, acceptance and forgiveness. It is important to slow down when we feel emotionally stressed, take some deep breaths and give ourselves time to process whatever is happening. We will remain out of balance if we try to ignore or repress stressful emotions. In this case, the only way out is in—into the heart of the emotion itself, so you can allow yourself to feel what is happening fully with no judgement or blame.

Physical balance falls into place with healthy diet and exercise, but these alone will not be enough. Both mental and emotional imbalance have a strong effect on the body's health and well-being. All of these aspects interact with each other, so paying close attention to balancing all three is essential to overall happiness.

When we are in a state of balance in mind, body and emotions, we open ourselves to the wholeness of our being. Our ability to enjoy life to the fullest is a natural outcome of overall balance. When in a balanced state of mind and heart, we are able to be our best selves, to live in a loving and harmonious way as we interact with those in our world.

Love is our essential nature and when we are balanced, there is no obstruction to loving behaviour. Our life becomes an effortless flow of harmonious actions.

A state of balance is a state of equilibrium. A state of equilibrium is being at peace with ourselves and everyone in our world. It also means we have the steadiness not to become thrown off the rails by challenging situations that come our way. Equilibrium gives us the presence of mind to determine the best approach to a challenging situation.

In my personal life during the sacred journey with my mother, we experienced many challenges towards the end when everything in her body appeared to go out of balance.

Journal entry, July 2011, Ellenton, Florida

We knew it was important to bring Mom back to a state of balance. A call to her doctor was necessary so that we could determine what had happened last night and do what was required to prevent another episode. Things felt very out of balance this morning. She just wanted to rest in her own bed, but we didn't want to take any risks. The doctor confirmed that what we had described sounded like a seizure and that she would need to be brought to the hospital for testing.

Mom agreed to go but insisted that we drive her rather than call an ambulance. The issue was lifting her up safely to transport her into the car. Once we got to the hospital, they would put her directly into a wheelchair upon our arrival. Lorrie and I felt our combined strength could handle it. Mom was not overweight, so together we lifted her from the bed to the walker and then to the car. This felt like a major accomplishment for which Mom was so grateful. To have an ambulance drive up to the house in full view of the neighbours would have devastated her.

Inner balance is essential for dealing with these challenges. I am always working on this. If I lose my balance, I start over. I can always start over. Maintaining balance requires resilience. If I remain aware of both my thoughts and emotions, I can navigate challenges by reflecting on what is needed, what is required of me and what actions to take. I become an aware witness to the upheaval around me. We can build resilience with daily reflection, focus and release of tension. This will enable us to discern the best course of action in any given situation.

For me, resilience means more than just bouncing back from adversity. Resilience certainly includes bouncing back, but I believe when we bounce back, we're not the same, we are stronger. In that strength we build a greater capacity to thrive as we create a more powerful and successful life. With resilience we create flexibility that can move with change and challenge while we bring forth our best selves. In this way, building resilience becomes one of the most practical things we can do for ourselves and our lives. We build resilience by creating balance in all areas of our lives.

Include balance in relationships

Everything in our life is about relationships. We have relationships with people, with our work, with our finances, with nature, with our pets, with our food and most importantly, with ourselves.

If a relationship is not flowing smoothly, something is out of balance. Sometimes communication is needed— listening and speaking the truth. There are other times when silence and having some quiet time to yourself is needed to restore balance in your relationship.

How much time you spend alone and how much time you spend with friends and family can be balanced with careful attention so that you can maintain your state of well-being. If we spend all our time attending to the needs of others, we become imbalanced. It is important to include yourself in the care and attention you give to each relationship.

Practising the art of balance

Meditation, prayer, slowing down and breathing deeply are effective tools for creating a balanced state of mind. There are many forms of meditation, and any one of them would be effective. It depends on what method you are drawn to and what works for you. Some forms of meditation can be active rather than passive, objective rather than subjective.

Examples of objective meditation include working in a garden, playing golf, walking meditation, swimming, playing music, and almost anything that requires your full focus. When you bring full attention to the activity at hand, the mind stops its endless random thoughts and is still, present and aware of the moment. This is being here now, the famous now moment. It is a matter of focused attention and maintaining that attention.

Deep meditation requires sitting comfortably with eyes closed, taking a dive into the depths of our being. The attention can be drawn inward with a focus on the breath, a mantra, an affirmative statement or even a word such as love, peace or God. Yoga postures or a brisk walk are excellent preparation for meditation and are a form of objective meditation. To go deep into the consciousness of our being requires sitting with eyes closed for at least twenty to thirty minutes. Sitting in meditation every day brings equanimity into our daily activity.

To bring strength to the focus of creating balance you can begin with statements of intention such as:

- Today, I am creating balance in every area of my life.
- I am balancing all aspects of my life—mental, emotional and physical.

- As I am balanced my capacity to enjoy life expands.
- I am creating balance within myself and my relationship with others.
- The more balanced I become the more joy I experience in every moment.
- I am so grateful for the experience of mental, physical and emotional balance.

Balance in society

Respecting the rights of others is a key to world peace. When human rights are violated, we all suffer in ways that ripple throughout our society, weakening our structures of peace, weakening our happiness and destroying harmonious connections that could enhance our prosperity and well-being. When human rights are nurtured and respected, we all benefit from the strength it brings to the whole of our society.

Throughout history, there have been a few misguided, confused leaders who propagated a lack of respect for life for their own selfish purposes. Lack of respect is a violation of our right to live in happiness as equals, sharing life under the same sun and sky and breathing the same air. It is a privilege to be alive. With awareness of this truth, we can build respect among our families, communities and nations. This is living with balance in an imbalanced world.

It is important for these times to gain a deeper understanding and appreciation of the importance of honouring human rights, understanding that will open our hearts to compassionate living because respecting the rights of others is living with compassion. It is a gift we can give to everyone we meet—compassion filled with much love, happiness and celebration. This is the most loving contribution we can make to our world.

To understand how you are imbalanced or balanced in your life, here are some reflections to ponder as you explore the experience of balance.

What areas of your life are in balance? How can you maintain that balance?

What areas of your life are out of balance? What changes do you need to make to restore balance to your mind, body and emotions? To your finances? To your work? To your diet?

Are your relationships balanced or imbalanced? What changes do you need to make to maintain balance in your relationships?

25

Silence

'See how nature—trees, flowers, grass—grows in silence, see the stars, the moon and the sun, how they move in silence . . . we need silence to be able to touch souls.'—Mother Teresa

In a state of balance, we can appreciate the silence within ourselves, the silence that also underlies everything in creation. We live in such a noisy world that it's hard to imagine how anything could be silent. How can we notice silence with so much noise?

In a world of opposites, silence exists simultaneous to noise. There is silence between the words that I am writing, the thoughts I am thinking. There is silence beneath the noise and in between sounds, like the silence between musical notes. There is a quick silent pause between each breath, each beat of our hearts. Silence is an infinite field of possibility, a blank white canvas waiting, content to be nothing other than it is.

Within the silence of the heart is peace. Within the silence of the mind is peace.

When the body is still and at rest, it is at peace. I love silence. Silence feeds my soul. Silence became a trusted friend when I found myself alone. Appreciating silence, I don't feel alone at all. I feel full and content. I enjoy paying a visit to this silent presence each day. Even when there are various noises on the outside, if I tune into the silence, I can experience stillness and peace.

In silence we experience our essential nature. Underneath the personality and the ego is a self that just is—in the silence underlying the play of life. In this silence, we are connected as one. This is a sacred space that exists within each of us. Bringing our attention to silence will serve to balance the noise of a chaotic world.

In relationships, there is a time to speak our truth and a time to remain silent. Maintaining this balance is essential to maintain a harmonious flow. Sometimes more is conveyed in silence. There are also times when no words are possible.

How can we know when to speak and when to remain silent? In a challenging situation, it is best to simply pause and then tune in to your heart. The wisdom of the heart will guide you to the best approach. I use this practice often and silently ask myself, 'how best to communicate right now?' The answers always come, or I get a feeling that it is best not to speak in that moment. If you are upset and are confused about when to speak out, you can wait until you settle down and then return to the conversation from a more balanced state of mind.

Forgiveness becomes possible while resting in a silent state of being. Retreating into silence can offer the opportunity to heal and recover as we allow the space for stuck emotions to surface. Letting go is an act of forgiveness. Releasing will free us up to heal from the past and move forward with increased resilience.

Journal entry, July 2011, Ellenton, Florida

We waited in silence for about two hours for Mom's test results to come back. Yes, she had had a seizure, we were told, but she had also had a silent heart attack and would need to stay overnight for observation. This was a surprise. Mom's comment was 'I just want to go home'. But she also wanted to build up her strength and felt she had no choice but to stay in the hospital.

We could see Mom's strength waning. She was no longer able to get up on her own to use the toilet. Nurses had to be called in to assist. What would happen if she were at home? Neither my sister nor I could safely lift her. The doctors were strangely silent about her prognosis and how long she would need to be in the hospital. In Mom's view, she was building up strength to go home. But was she? What was really happening?

The next recommendation was for her to have an MRI to look at her brain since she had had a seizure. We wondered if she could withstand the MRI; she seemed so weak. I had to know the truth—if this was the end, shouldn't she be told? If recovery was not possible, we all needed to know. What was the point in putting her through more procedures that would tax her strength? Within the silence of the hospital room, these questions were demanding answers.

I pulled a nurse to the side and asked her point-blank—is Mom going to recover? What is the prognosis? She said it didn't look good, but a doctor would have to confirm. Once confirmed, she could go to the hospice, which was a much nicer environment for the final days left to her.

Later that day, the doctor came in to tell Mom that more treatments were not going to cure her at this point. The cancer in her brain was causing seizures so it wasn't safe to go home, and if she couldn't get up on her own, she would need to have nurses available around the clock. Mom's response was 'I just want to go home'. We wanted so much to grant her wish but even the nurse said she had tried taking care of her brother in a similar situation and would never recommend that we try it ourselves.

That night Mom was transported to the hospice down the road from her neighbourhood. Once she was settled into her room, she was silent most of the time. She did not speak much in her final days. We don't know what she was thinking or feeling about what was happening as she was absorbing the finality of her life. No words could describe how she must have felt, and we did not have the words to convey how we were feeling as we sat with her each day in silence. The only words that felt appropriate at the end were 'Thank you Mom' and 'I love you Mom'.

Practising the art of silence

In the quiet of the morning is the ideal time to begin the day with silence. It is a time to reflect on our dreams, our intentions for the day, release negative thoughts and feelings to clear the space for wisdom in our choices through the day.

- Today, I am open to increasing my experience of silence.
- I am allowing silent spaces to come to the forefront throughout this day.
- I respect the silent dignity of life within myself and in everyone I meet.

In this way we choose to begin the day with a balanced heart and mind. From a state of balance we easily bring forth our strengths and gifts as we interact with those in our world.

The evening is an ideal time for silent reflection.

What worked well today? What did not work and how could you have handled it differently?

Did you experience silence today? Were you challenged to notice the silence beneath the noise?

What did you discover about silence? What did you discover about yourself in relation to silence?

Were you able to embrace silence or did you find ways to avoid silence?

'Be quiet a lot and speak little—and silence will come in your heart, and your spirit will be calm and full of peace.'—Saint Seraphim of Sarov

26

Trust

*'Self-trust is the first secret of success.'—Ralph Waldo
Emerson*

I have learnt to trust life itself as the ultimate teacher.
I have opened myself to the learning that each experience
brings. People come and go—some can be trusted; others
cannot. Situations change when people's minds or feelings
change. I cannot control that, so there is no use trusting in
factors beyond my control.

If self-trust is the secret of success, then how can we
learn self-trust? To trust in ourselves, we can begin with
tuning into the wisdom of the heart because the mind will
always be full of doubt. The mind will always question
everything. Questions are good—they can lead us to greater
clarity and understanding, but the truthful answers must
come from within. To get to the truthful answers, we must
access the heart's wisdom.

The easiest way to do this is to sit quietly in a place you won't be interrupted. Take a deep breath and exhale slowly. As you breathe in, imagine your breath flowing in through your heart. Exhale slowly through the heart. Once you are relaxed, quietly ask yourself, 'What does my heart want to tell me about . . . (whatever situation or challenge you would like some clarity on). Just sit quietly with your eyes closed and continue breathing in and out through the heart. After five to ten minutes, write down what comes to you without effort. I have received many insights in this way—it works every time.

At times of great challenge, trusting in the heart's wisdom can become our refuge. I experienced this at a time of great loss. Learning to accept the reality that unfolds before us each day is learning to trust that the experiences life brings to us offer the opportunity to learn about ourselves and how to choose our responses for the best possible outcomes. We are not at the mercy of our circumstances—we are at the mercy of our own choices.

It is so easy not to trust. Life often takes unexpected twists and turns. People change their minds; lovers change their feelings, they have a 'change of heart', which leaves us disappointed, heartbroken and alone. People sometimes lie to us and create deceptions, both personal and professional. The more we trust in ourselves, the more we are not influenced by others' lies and deceptions.

I have found that when I consistently choose love, I am led to people, circumstances and experiences that generate love. Love is respectful, truthful and kind. When I release resentment, judgement, desire for revenge or retaliation, my heart opens to giving and receiving love. Once I trust in the choice of love, I know that which is most needed will come forth. A self-loving response is to stand in my own truth, speak my truth and remain steadfast in what is best for me and my life.

When Alan and Naomi were killed, I surrendered my trust to the process of life itself. At the time, I had no other choice because I would not have been able to survive the loss. I chose to go deeply into the emotions that came up from the loss. That is when I discovered that there will never be a loss of love. Love is an infinite resource waiting to be tapped, to be embraced, to be included as an essential part of life. I can trust in love to restore balance, to repair a broken heart, to inspire new perspectives, to open my eyes to a new vision of possibility.

In a slow-motion death, such as cancer, there is a process of dying as the body begins to shut down. I learnt about trusting in this process in order to be at peace with the loss of my mother when she was dying of lung cancer. Trusting from the heart brings the power of peace.

Journal entry, July 2011, Ellenton, Florida

We were taking each day at a time, trusting in the hospice staff, trusting in Mom to come to a state of peace, trusting in our ability to support her transition with love, and letting go of our own fears about the dying process.

My dad flew in from Arizona the next day. Both my sons were now here. Both my brothers flew in, not knowing if and when Mom was going to die. They could only take a week off work but decided that they would rather see Mom for the last time while she was alive before she lost consciousness than wait for a memorial service after she had passed.

Trust is essential to our relationships. What about our relationship to life? Can I trust in the experience that life brings to me even as it slips away?

Mom woke from her nap this afternoon and said, 'I'm afraid to ask the Lord to take me. Call the priest.' I had never heard her talk like this before. She had converted to Catholicism when she married my father. She hadn't been to church in years. But there we were by her bedside, and that was what she was asking. Father Jose Garcia was called in to perform the last rites. My father, brothers, sister and I gathered around my mother's bed, holding hands as the priest said some prayers, sprinkled holy water, anointed her forehead with oil and gave us all holy communion. It was a ritual that served to unify us in that moment and to unify my mother with her inner spirit, which is beyond death, and which is the essence of life, animating the human experience in this body.

We chose to trust in the peace that death would bring to my mother. There was no doubt about that. She would rest in peace and that brought some comfort to us in those final days.

What do we mean by being trustworthy? Building trust is essential in any relationship. Being a trustworthy person is necessary for success in work, friendships and marriage. How can we become more trustworthy?

To treat others as we would want to be treated is being trustworthy. Honouring our agreements is being trustworthy. Listening deeply is being trustworthy. Being accepting, forgiving and inclusive is being trustworthy.

When we choose to accept rather than to judge we are being compassionate. Speaking the truth is being trustworthy. If you want to have trusting relationships, become the trustworthy person you would like to see in others. How we interact with each other determines our success. Trust is essential to successful relationships in all areas of our life. Building trust takes time, patience, communication and attention. Creating balance in relationships requires trust.

We can increase our ability to be trustworthy and deepen our friendships as a result. Our relationships will become more stable and mutually fulfilling.

To strengthen your focus on becoming trustworthy and learning to trust others, here are some statements of intention to get you started. You can add some of your own that pertain to your individual life.

- I am open to becoming more trusting of others and myself.
- I am willing to let go and trust. I am learning to trust life as it unfolds.
- As I increase my trust, my heart opens to the full experience of life.
- I trust and watch as each moment unfolds perfectly.

Much insight can be gained by reflecting on our experience of self-trust and how this plays out in our trust for others.

How many ways can you let go and trust?

Where did your resistance show up with regard to trust?

Who do you trust? What do you trust? Can you trust yourself?

Can you be open to trusting the experiences that life brings you as opportunities for gaining wisdom and learning how to love?

What did you learn about yourself as you explored your experience of trust?

27

Selfless Service

'That service is noblest when rendered for its own sake.'
—Mohandas K. Gandhi

Giving without expectation of anything in return is selfless service. Giving can take the form of sharing food, resources, money or time. It can manifest as acts of kindness or it can also take the form of extending love without condition, without the need for reciprocity. This happens naturally in a state of surrender.

Developing trust will lead you to a state of surrender. Not surrender to another person but surrender to the heart of life and what is happening moment to moment—meeting life with your heart with unconditional acceptance. This is true selfless service. To enhance the experience of being alive, we must surrender with an open heart, setting aside ego, judgement and division so that we may create connection and collaboration. This is selfless service. In a state of selfless surrender, it becomes natural to treat others as we would want to be treated. This is giving and receiving love in a way that is the most appropriate.

One of the most empowering ways to serve someone is to give him or her your undivided attention. In this way you are honouring them with your presence as you give the gift of deep listening.

We also serve our immediate environment by keeping it clean and not wasting resources. My son Adam noticed that there was a lot of trash along some of the roads in his part of the city. So, when he takes his daily walk with his dog Romeo, he takes a trash bag with him. As he walks along, he simply picks up the trash, and at the end of the walk, puts it in a large garbage bin. He serves his neighbourhood without being asked on a daily basis. This is selfless service.

In some communities, selfless service is part of their spiritual practice. Food and shelter are provided to those in need. Volunteering without expectation of recognition or reward is selflessly serving the community. Communities thrive when selfless service is active and consistent because something much greater is contributed to the welfare of all. The whole is greater than the sum of its parts.

We contribute to our wholeness when we serve selflessly. We become wholehearted human beings when love is shared without measure.

Practising the art of selfless service

Selfless service is a powerful practice to set aside selfish agendas and ego. There are numerous ways in which to serve each day. In the stillness of the morning, as you sit quietly to prepare for your day, simply ask, 'How can I serve today?' Let go and trust that opportunities to serve will come forth in abundance once you set your intention.

- Today, I am open to the experience of selfless service.
- I am willing to serve with respect as I open my heart to the love that is present in each moment.
- I serve myself when I serve others. I open myself to the sacred gift of selfless service as I connect unselfishly with those in my world.
- I am so grateful for the experience of unconditional love that is happening in this moment.

To begin the day with an intention to give and receive love without conditions is a sacred gift.

To explore selfless service in your life, take some time to reflect on how you can explore ways to serve that are beneficial to yourself and others.

What are some ways you provided selfless service today?

Did you experience resistance or challenge in regard to selfless service?

Were you able to create a breakthrough? What was your experience?

Did you notice a sense of peace and contentment in the process of service?

When put into practice, selfless service will deepen our connection to the greater good of humanity as it opens our minds and expands our hearts.

28

Peace

'There is no way to peace—peace is the way.'—A.J. Muste

After the Mumbai terrorist attack I didn't think peace would ever be possible for me. For the past eleven years I had been living an ideal, peaceful life with my family in a meditation sanctuary. Our daily lives were dedicated to creating inner peace and teaching meditation to others so they too could experience the peace that resides in all of us. And then this world came crashing down.

I understood that true peace comes from within our own being, and we bring peace to our world when we are at peace with ourselves. Peace is always possible. I knew this, but when the extreme opposite of peace happened to my family, I felt as if I had been tossed out of a secure womb and into a dark uncertainty with no end in sight. Where was peace? Where was love?

I was offered a refuge from deep within my soul and that was forgiveness. If love was lacking, could I bring love back by forgiving? What would that mean? Who would I forgive and why would it matter? I did not know the answers to these questions, but I knew love would override hatred. Forgiveness would serve as the bridge back to peace.

It's so hard to accept that Alan and Naomi died in the way that they did. It was as if they were killed in a war. The city of Mumbai considered the terrorist attack an act of war. It was a war on humanity fuelled by a total lack of regard for human life. What was the point of it all? There were no winners of this war, only losers. Life was destroyed violently with no regard for our shared humanity. The ripple effect of this attack created waves of pain, suffering, grief, anger, hatred for the so-called enemy, distrust and disunity. The negative waves go on and on. But something else was born out of this darkness.

There is a light of love that resides in the human heart. It can be clouded over, but I don't think it ever goes out. When messages of love came pouring in from around the world—messages from people of all religions—I knew peace was possible.

Forgiveness and peace go hand in hand. I was amazed to discover an entire organization that collects and shares stories of forgiveness from around the world. On a visit to London, I had the opportunity to hear Marina Cantacuzino, founder of the London-based Forgiveness Project, astutely sum up what is necessary in order to forgive.

To forgive seems to involve the following:

- Reconciling with that which is painful or unresolved. In other words, making peace with what you can't change.
- It also involves a refusal to dehumanize the 'other'. A recognition perhaps of what the American poet Longfellow said: 'If we could read the secret history of our enemies, we would find in each person's life sorrow and suffering enough to disarm all hostility.'
- In friendships and intimate relationships, it's about giving up the presumption that people should behave as we expect and want them to. David Whyte, the poet-philosopher, said, 'All Friendships of any length are based on continued mutual forgiveness.' Forgiveness, I've long thought, is the oil of personal relationships.
- In crimes that are unspeakable, it's not about forgiving the act but about forgiving humanity (of which we are a part) for its fallibility and for failing. My favourite description of forgiveness has been attributed to the author Mark Twain who said: 'Forgiveness is the fragrance that the violet sheds on the heel that has crushed it.'
  I like that because it shows forgiveness grows out of damage (pain is the great motivator to forgive). That it's messy. But that it's also potentially a healing balm.

As Marina says, 'Making peace with what you can't change' is the first step towards forgiveness. This is proactive acceptance. Acceptance is necessary to truly listen and come to an understanding of what happened. We may never agree with it, but agreement is not required for forgiveness. We may never understand a person's actions, but we can come to a place of acceptance, however heartbreaking. Yes, it can be messy, but it is ultimately healing.

There are so many inspiring stories of forgiveness that have transformed lives. If you want to read some of these stories and learn more about all the ways in which people have forgiven and how it affected their lives, the Forgiveness Project (theforgivenessproject.com) has interviewed over 160 people and organized these stories on their website according to various themes. Reading these stories can help you open your heart to prepare for choosing forgiveness in your own life.

There can be no inner peace without forgiveness. There will be no peace in our families without forgiveness. Without peace in our families, there will be no peace in our world.

To understand peace, we must experience peace from the inside out.

Peace metrics, the way to a more compassionate society

I first learnt about the Global Peace Index in 2012 at a conference in Washington D.C. hosted by the Institute for Economics and Peace (www.economicsandpeace.org). After having spent the past three years exploring effective ways to create an environment for positive change, I reached out to educators, businesspeople and government leaders. I found this information an exciting revelation, as I knew it would provide a way to make a more compelling case to implement peace-building programmes. When I began talking about the Global Peace Index in India, eyes opened and ears pricked up as soon as Mumbaikars learnt that India ranked 142 out of 158 countries. 'We are a people of peace—we can do much better than that!' was a comment I often heard. From that point on, One Life Alliance became a global peace initiative whose mission is to collaborate with educators, business, government and like-minded NGOs to raise the peace index all over the world. As one of the speakers stated at an American University conference on peace economics and the role of business, 'What can be measured, can be improved.'

At the conference, I learnt about the role of business in creating a foundation for peace.

Peace is one of the most used words in the English language, and it means different things to different people. Therefore, peace is intangible and often left to the realm of the new age, the spiritual or religious. What about peace in everyday life? Can the focus of increasing peace benefit business? What would that look like for a society? When community problems are resolved, life is in balance, and we all enjoy more peace. Trust, cooperation and inclusiveness are necessary to resolve conflicts, both personally and in our society.

But what drives society? It is economics—money—that moves and shapes our societies. Isn't that what drove the terrorists to join the terrorist training camp run by Lashkar-e-Taiba? What if they had learnt of other choices that would educate them in other ways to provide financial support?

Business can play an important and essential role by engaging in new ways to build structures of peace. Education, business and government can increase their understanding of conflict management to develop competency in strengthening relationships with each other and reaching out to the disadvantaged members of society.

When the peace metrics of a community are understood, it becomes clear what areas need balance, integration and resilience. Businesses can work with consultants and NGOs to steer stability initiatives towards community-based programmes.

The Institute for Economics and Peace has done a brilliant job outlining a clear way to understand the practical aspects of creating positive peace and what that requires.

The three main components to create 'pillars of peace' are:

- A sound business environment
- A well-functioning government
- Equal distribution of resources

The five main components to create these are:

- Free flow of information
- Quality education
- Respecting the rights of others
- Low levels of corruption
- Good relations with neighbours

It is obvious that balance is the key, and it takes all aspects
of a society working together in collaboration to maintain
that balance. When economies become unstable, fear and
violence increase. When governments are corrupt, the
distribution of the resources that are required to survive
and prosper is not addressed effectively or in some cases,
not at all.

Many examples of 'what's good for humanity can be
good for business' were given at this conference by graduate
students who presented papers on this research. There is a
strong consensus that business can be a positive driver of
peace while contributing to the economic stability of the
community.

Business can be a force for war or peace—both can be
financially profitable for business, but peace is by far the
sustaining factor in creating maximum profit and personal
enrichment when people organize for a collective purpose
to respond to social needs.

At the end of two days of intense focus on this subject,
I realized that what is really fuelling this research and the
resulting peace initiatives is love—love and compassion
for humanity. This research shows us how connected and
interdependent we are, and thus, how important it is to
find new ways to work together.

Raising the peace index first in ourselves gives rise to
a stronger motivation to address the structures of peace
to raise the peace index in our communities. We cannot
eliminate acts of terror and other violent crimes, but we can
strengthen ourselves and our world through engagement
and increased understanding about the economics of peace
and how this contributes to our well-being and progress.

Each of us has the potential to move in the direction of peace or violence. How will we respond in each moment of our lives? How can we adapt to challenging situations to bring about a response that is respectful of the dignity of life in all? These are questions that require joining together in new ways to find new answers.

The basis of inner peace is a calm, contented mind. To relax the mind and body it is helpful to spend at least fifteen to twenty minutes a day in quiet contemplation or deep meditation.

To create peace in the heart and mind, you can use these affirmations to guide your experience:

Here and now, in this moment, I am experiencing the serenity of inner peace.

May I forgive all. May all forgive me. In this way may peace fill my heart and flow into my life.

I am open to the experience of peace flowing into my life in each moment throughout this day.

In the stillness of my heart is peace.

I am whole and at peace with myself. I am at peace with all and everyone.

In this moment, peace permeates each breath and each beat of my heart.

In love and gratitude I celebrate the experience of inner and outer peace.

A peaceful heart brings forth love. Love is the greatest contribution we can make. Forgiveness is an act of self-love. Learning to love myself is what has helped to heal my life as I move forward. Forgiveness is a necessary ingredient to restore peace within myself. In this way, I bring peace into the world.

29

Compassion

'When your fear touches someone's pain, it becomes pity. When your love touches someone's pain, it becomes compassion.'—Stephen Levine

Compassion is the result of a forgiving heart. Compassion is an extension of love. Forgiveness itself is compassion. Love feels compassion for those in pain. Love forgives those who forgot their connection and disregarded another human being's dignity with abuse or violence. To respond with compassion enables us to meet life at its centre, right at the heart, however messy, however challenging. Compassion is patience, silence, acceptance, listening deeply and understanding that life includes both happiness and suffering.

Compassion in Cheetah Camp, Mumbai

For several Sundays in the spring of 2012, Sameer, my regular Mumbai cab driver, drove me to the Cheetah Camp slum to join a group of students from St Andrew's for an education project. This was part three of the One Life Alliance pledge that a group of twelve students had taken the previous December. They were part of an interfaith group at St Andrew's College—Catholics, Hindus and Muslims—who had pledged to honour the sacredness of life in both self and others for thirty days and then plan a project to put this into practice in the community. They chose to bring quality education to students in the Cheetah Camp slum—maths, computer skills, English and cooking—all practical additions to the standard government school curriculum.

On Sunday, their one day off each week, St Andrew's volunteers and a hundred Cheetah Camp students of all ages met in a big schoolroom to enrich their education. Except for the English class, everything was taught in Hindi, so I sat and listened while watching the enthusiastic faces and smiles of everyone in the room. I had never seen students so excited to be in a classroom. I don't remember ever feeling excited in school. I took it for granted and often felt bored, just waiting to get through the day. These students were eager. There were constant questions and lots of laughter. None of them had been forced to be there. They chose to be there and were having fun learning new skills.

I was sitting next to a little girl named Anjun. She enjoyed practising her English by asking me questions. 'Are you married? Do you have children?' I hesitated, then decided to tell her the truth about what happened to my husband and daughter. Her eyes opened wide. 'Oh, that's very bad! I wish to kill the terrorist.'

'Oh no,' I replied, 'we need to teach them how to love, to honour the sacredness of life in ourselves and in each other like we're doing here.'

'What was your daughter's name?' Anjun asked. 'When is her birthday?' It just so happened that the following Friday was Naomi's birthday. Before the class ended, Anjun asked for my phone number. I gave it to her and then forgot all about it, as the week ahead was busy with many meetings. Friday was a tender day, full of Naomi memories, sadness, a fusion of grief and love. It was 10 p.m., and I was falling asleep when my phone rang.

'Hello ma'am, this is Anjun.'

'Anjun! Hello! What a nice surprise. How are you?'

'Isn't today your daughter's birthday?'

I was stunned. 'Yes,' I answered slowly, feeling my heart swell, 'it is.'

'I'm calling to wish your daughter a happy birthday. Please don't cry, ma'am.'

Anjun is ten years old. She lives with her three siblings and parents in a ten-by-ten-foot makeshift hut on the outskirts of town. On the first day we met, she invited me to her home for lunch. On the following Sunday I walked with her during our lunch hour down alleyways filled with people washing clothes in large buckets, sleeping dogs, goats, children playing or helping their mothers sweep their small doorways. Anjun proudly escorted me into their small hut and introduced me to her parents and siblings. Her father brought in a plastic chair and insisted I sit down while her mother brought me tea. In this small space, they managed to have everything they needed. Along one side was a wooden counter that had a gas stove, a big bucket for washing dishes and clothes, a small refrigerator, and even a small television mounted on the wall. There were mats and pillows stacked on a shelf at the back of the hut. The five of them slept on the floor, ate on the floor and spent the rest of their day outside the hut. Inside, the hut was spotless and well organized. Anjun's mother made masala dosas and dal for our lunch. The food was cooked to perfection, absolutely delicious. No one else in the family spoke English, so we communicated with smiles and hand gestures. A warm and friendly connection was made without words. I left the Cheetah Camp with a happy heart that day.

I was amazed that Anjun remembered what day it was on the following Friday, Naomi's birthday. And I was so touched that she thought to give me a call. It was almost like a message from Naomi herself. That brief phone call is a treasure I will never forget.

There were many gifts shared and received on those Sundays at Cheetah Camp. What I observed the most was the inclusion of whatever life was presenting—whether it was a new friend, people of different religious beliefs, race and education—all were accepted without judgement. People shared what they had with each other and offered their homes to visitors with welcoming smiles. This was simply a part of their culture, inherent in how they were raised and how they lived day to day. It was a blessing to experience this so intimately during those few weeks. In my country we live much further apart, have less contact and less opportunity for day-to-day sharing. I know the people in Cheetah Camp have their own challenges and life is not always so peaceful and happy. But at first glance, it is refreshing to see the harmony that exists in the midst of this diverse community.

On the long cab ride back to the Trident Hotel that Sunday I felt myself relaxing into a simple feeling of joy. I was blessed to be included in this community, even for a short time.

Practising the art of compassion

There are times in life when compassion is called for, when compassion is the most appropriate response to an unexpected challenge. The COVID-19 pandemic has affected nearly everyone across the world. It has become a time to slow down, do less, take a break from routine and, most importantly, to stay home. It is a time to consider others as much as ourselves. It is a time for self-compassion and compassion for everyone around us as we wash our hands and wipe everything down with disinfectant. Not from fear but from love for life. We accept this reality and do our part to contain it as much as we can. This is respecting the dignity of life in ourselves and in each other. This is loving life so much we will change our routines and inconvenience ourselves out of consideration for our neighbours. This is practising the art of compassion in daily life. Times like these call for increased compassion.

May we open to becoming more compassionate with ourselves and with each other. Compassion will increase the flow of love and will open our hearts as it provides comfort, support and closer connections.

Speaking or writing out these intentions will strengthen the experience of compassion as you open your heart with these words:

- Here and now, in this moment, I am opening to the experience of compassion.
- First and foremost, I am compassionate with myself. I love and accept myself as I am.
- I am compassionate with everyone I meet. I accept, include and forgive myself and others with compassion.
- I am compassion . . . I am . . . all is . . . one.
- I am so grateful for the experience of compassion that is happening here and now.
- I joyfully carry this compassionate focus with me throughout my day.

To ground your experience of compassion, here are some reflections you can write out in your journal to gain insight on this tender experience of love as it continues to grow in your life.

What opportunities did you have today to be compassionate? Were you able to let go of judgement and choose compassion?

Did you observe compassion in others? Were others compassionate towards you?

Could you be compassionate with yourself?

What was most challenging in regard to flowing compassion?

30

Love

'There are four questions of value in life ... What is sacred?
Of what is the spirit made? What is worth living for and
what is worth dying for? The answer to each is the same ...
only love.'—Don Juan DeMarco

In essence, every chapter in this book has been about
love. We have explored twenty-nine ways to be loving
to yourself and others. Practise any one of these and you
will increase your experience of love. There are an infinite
number of ways to give and receive love. We have touched
upon just a few, but if you start with these, you will be
well on your way to living from your heart as you bring
more love into the world. I have discovered that love is
the most abundant resource we have as human beings,
both to give and to receive.

Love does not reject us—we tend to reject love. How
is this possible? If we are only looking at the surface of the

situation, it appears that someone else is to blame. After all, someone is not loving us or has taken love away from us. So we blame them. We judge them. We close the door to our hearts and lock them out. We lose trust in them. We may even lose trust in life. After that, we are more careful about opening up to let love in. If we're willing to look deeper into the situation to find what is true about love, we must look deeper into ourselves. Does love really come from someone else? Who is it that is experiencing love? Isn't it yourself? Did someone else open you up and put love inside you? Not possible!

Who is it that holds the key to your heart? Who has the power to lock it up or open it wide? Did you give that key away? Do you want to get it back?

It took the sudden, violent death of my husband and thirteen-year-old daughter to teach me the truth about love. And this was the most painful and yet most powerful lesson I have ever learnt. This was no fairy tale, it was the hard edge of reality. But first, I had to experience a loss that took my whole outer life away. I am still here but the rest was gone. Overnight. So what was left? Could I change this reality? The only reality I have the power to change is my own thought process and the actions I take based on my choices.

Love itself is not a thought, but our minds colour our thoughts and beliefs and that is what colours our experience of life. Love abides in an ever-flowing stream, permeating every cell of our being, every breath, each beat of our heart. I learnt to access this love, to invite the experience of love with acceptance, inclusion, forgiveness, trust, compassion and gratitude. This is just the beginning. Once the gates are open, we can amplify the love by connecting with others, listening to our inner voice, listening to others with our full attention, sharing our thoughts and feelings honestly, being patient with self and others, having fun, laughing, singing, dancing and so much more. If we hold on to blame, judgement, exclusion, distance, fear, distrust, anger, resentment, guilt, regret—what are we choosing?

We are rejecting love when we lock ourselves up, such as avoiding people who have hurt us, not sharing our feelings, holding on to resentment and anger and pretending not to care. Love is ever inviting, ever-present, patient, flowing, accepting. Are you willing?

When I accepted my negative thoughts and feelings with compassion, embraced them for what they were and simply returned them to the whole of my being, no longer choosing that experience, I began to experience love in abundance, in a way I never knew was possible. That is now a choice I make each day.

Love is never lost once we find our true selves. What is true is what is at the core of our being. Our inner truth is the foundation of our experience, our essence—never changing, like the depths of the ocean. It is the 'you' beneath the ever-changing happenings of life. Consciousness, awareness, presence, all of these are terms for that 'you', that 'I' that is the ground of your being. When Socrates so wisely advised 'know thyself', this is the self he was referring to. When Polonius advised Hamlet 'to thine own self be true', this is the self he meant. When we reject love, we are rejecting this self. This is the most painful rejection of all. When we embrace this self, we are embracing love.

How else do we reject love? Making fun of something we fear is pushing away that experience as we hide behind the mask of humour. This is opting out of love—skimming the surface but never exploring the depths. We have free will. Just know that one choice leads to another, and outcomes are based on choices. What outcome do you choose? To move beyond the ordinary into the realm of the extraordinary requires both feet in, along with heart and mind. It is trusting in love to guide the way to the next choice and the next, always expanding your experience of yourself as you explore life to the fullest.

Love guides the way, even in death.

Journal entry, 19 July 2011

I stayed overnight at the hospice because I could hear Mom's breaths getting further apart. At 4 a.m. I was wide awake, so I got up and sat down next to her bed, held her hand for a moment, but that felt intrusive, so I let go, just sitting in silence, listening, feeling the soft energy envelop us. After a while, her breath stopped. Just like that. I sat in this stillness for about half an hour before informing the nurse. Then I called my sister who contacted the rest of the family. The sun was just beginning to rise over the meadow. Each of my children was born at sunrise. I remember feeling an intense euphoric love when I held each of them in my arms for the first time. What I felt as I watched this sunrise was a different kind of love. It was sweet, sacred and peaceful, the ending of the dark night and dawning of a new day.

Love is the connection between life and death. Love is what keeps us connected to those who have died. Love connects us to life itself. Love is woven throughout life, intersecting our thoughts, actions, relationships. It's not from dust we come and to dust we return—it's love from the beginning and to the end, the first and last gift of life.

Practising the art of love

If you are reading this book, you have shown some openness of heart and mind. If you have applied any of these chapters to your daily life, you are practising the art of love. Every choice we make can give love or deny love. When we choose to give love, we add to the fullness of life in ourselves and others. When we choose to deny love, we close the door to our hearts.

Our choices affect more than just ourselves. We are interconnected and can influence the world around us with every choice we make. This is a big responsibility and contains great power, the best kind of power, the power that increases love and serves to evolve our experience as it expands our hearts.

Practising the art of love is learning to love ourselves as we are, accepting all aspects of ourselves. This includes blessing our past—experiences that showed us who we are and who we are not as we made various choices. We may choose differently now that we have reflected upon who we are now and what we value.

When choosing through the lens of love, we naturally want to bring value to ourselves and others. We want to uplift, inspire and support those around us in whatever way we can in that circumstance. We learn to recognize that which does not serve us or will not support our growth as we increase our experience of love and peace. We learn to recognize the inner wolf that hides in the shadows, waiting to sabotage our progress.

Remember the wolf that lives inside of us? Which wolf will you feed? This is the inner self that contains both negative and positive polarities. Here is a way to heal the inner self so that we are not subject to being ruled by fear, anger and judgement. This is a form of self-terrorism that we can shift with conscious intention.

Transforming the inner self with love and acceptance

Step one is to first meet the inner self face to face. Acknowledge this vulnerable aspect of yourself. We all contain a mix of positive and negative qualities, thoughts and feelings. Accept this as being human and deserving of even more love. Forgive yourself for the times you were not loving with yourself or others. The fact that you feel sorry about this now shows how loving you really are. There is more goodness in you than any of the other stuff. We've all waded in muddy waters and even thrown a few mud balls. With forgiveness we can wash ourselves clean and begin again with a fresh open heart. We can begin a new loving relationship with ourselves and extend more love to others. The way we interact with others will begin to shift as love begins to flow in new ways.

I invite you to meet your inner self with compassion. Imagine a quiet sacred space that is safe and private. Invite your inner self to come forward. There is nothing to hide and nothing to be ashamed of because you are now rising above whatever hurt you and caused you to hurt others.

Ask yourself, 'What needs to be felt and healed in this moment?' 'What needs to be embraced and released?' If you are willing to let go, just relax and allow whatever is there to surface. Can you meet it with love? This is the higher aspect of yourself meeting the egoic self. Your higher self will always choose love. The ego is also a part of who we are; we don't have to let it dominate our lives. We can meet it with love and compassion.

Let's dive deeper to explore and transform the parts of us that close up and hold us back from giving and receiving love.

What does your inner critic look like? Note how it plays out in your life:

How does it limit you?
Self-sabotage?
Doubt?
Fear?
Anger?
Procrastination?
Blame?
Excuses?
Illness?
Avoidance?
Criticism, sarcasm, judgement?
Exclusion?
Ridicule?
Depression?

Write down specific incidents where you noticed these patterns or any other negative attitude or behaviour playing out and how it held you back from feeling happy, successful, healthy and abundant.

When you are able to transform the inner terrorist you have increased your ability to bring forth the truth of who you are with no limitation.

Surviving the death of a loved one requires resilience. Surviving heartbreak, surviving the death of a husband, a child or a close friend requires deep resilience that is built over time.

No matter what type of loss we are experiencing, our heart will feel shattered, broken and beyond emotional repair. But I learnt that the heart is miraculous and resilient. The heart is capable of healing and will emerge stronger than ever. The heart itself will help the healing process if we allow it to feel the loss thoroughly and completely. Allowing yourself to feel this takes love, compassion and patience. Resilience is built upon these beautiful gifts of the heart.

In order to access these gifts, which are actually practical tools, you must slow down and take the time to reflect and acknowledge what has happened and how you feel. Release from the emotional pain will eventually come, but first there will need to be acceptance and forgiveness of a life event we cannot change. It has already happened, and now we have a choice as to how we will respond and move forward. Or not. This too is a choice.

I came to realize the power of choice after Alan and Naomi were killed. In the immediate aftermath of the terrorist attack, I could choose to hate or I could choose to love. I chose love. How love has played out in my life has been the journey of my new life after my old life died along with Alan and Naomi. By choosing love, a new path was laid out, my personal 'yellow brick road' that would bring me home to myself.

I learnt that love comes in many forms, and each day I choose love I open myself to one of those forms of love. On some days love shows up as patience. On other days love requires forgiveness, acceptance and understanding. Love is what builds the resilience of the heart. I found it simplifies life to choose to be loving and open to how that may show up each day. When I embrace whatever form of love is required of me, I also allow myself to receive love in that form. This is the most powerful spiritual practice I have ever done after over forty years of daily meditation. It turns out that love meditation is not sitting with eyes closed, it is living life, embracing life and allowing love to fill my life with its gifts.

To set your inner compass to Love, here is a simple meditation to strengthen your love focus for the day.

Quietly repeat these statements as you allow your attention to settle into your heart:

- Here and now, in this moment, I am open to increasing my experience of love.
- I am love, I am loving, I love myself as I am in each new moment.
- Love is my true nature. I will honour the oneness and sacredness of life by being loving with myself and others.
- Love is life, life is love, I am . . . all is . . . love.
- I am so grateful for the experience of love that is happening here and now.

- I joyfully carry this loving focus with me throughout my day.

There is no completion to love, so there is no conclusion to this book about love. This book was meant to open your heart to love in simple ways. This is an ongoing process that will continue on and on as you live each day. The final words are inspired words of love.

This beautiful poem by Akbar Ahmed, academic, author, poet, playwright, filmmaker and former diplomat, sums up the essence of life's greatest gift and ultimate value—love.

What is it that I seek?
A force of such might
it sets me free
A light so bright
it blinds me
I heard it in the voice of the nightingale
I know it was in the hearts of the wise
I sensed it in the lover's tale
I saw it in your eyes
I heard it in Rumi's poetry
I know it was in Gandhi's gaze
I sensed it in Mandela's oratory
I saw it in Jesus' ways
What is this riddle and what is its part?
What is this enigma and mystery?
What can reveal the secrets of the heart
What has the power to change me?
It is God's greatest gift

It raises us high above
It is the ridge over the rift
It is love, love, love
Give it in generous measure
Give it as if there's no tomorrow
Give to all you meet this treasure
Give it and banish sorrow.

As you go forth into your life each day, may you remember that love is ready to flow in abundance. We each hold this treasure. When we share our love, it increases and only then we know the highest value of life.

Acknowledgements

Where to begin? There are so many people who inspired, contributed, supported and whose presence in my life made this book possible.

First of all, thank you to Raageshwari Loomba who connected me with Milee Ashwarya from Penguin Random House India. Thank you Milee for encouraging me to send in a book proposal and then accepting it! Thank you to my first editor, Roshini Dadlani. Roshini's keen eye and astute comments helped me to bring focus to parts of the book that needed polishing. I was then blessed with my second editor, Nicholas Rixon, whose enthusiasm washed away my doubts and gave me the validation I needed that we were on the right track. I also thank my copy editor Shreya Dhawan for her astute eye for detail.

A special thank you to Will Wilkinson, my writing coach, guide and mentor whose creative enthusiasm showed me what was possible and how to go about it as

I found my writing voice and finally expressed in writing from my heart and soul.

I gratefully acknowledge the friends I made in Mumbai, especially the Sachdeva family—Santosh, Gautam, Nikki and Shibani—the weekly meditations in your home kept me sane in the maximum city!

Thank you to Sarla Parekh whose loving and generous presence provided comfort for lunch each day. I knew I was not alone and appreciated your friendship and all the people I met through your introductions.

Thank you to the provider of my Mumbai home away from home—Mr P.R.S. Oberoi. Without your generosity I would not have come back to life in the magical city of Mumbai whose spirit shines bright throughout every storm. And thank you Mr Devendra Bharma for making my comings and goings over six years to the Trident so seamless and welcoming.

Thank you to all friends and family members who provided their homes when I was in a transitional period during the writing process. My dear father, Gary DeLisle, living in your house in Florida helped me get back on my feet after years of travelling. Nigel Lang—your charming home in Canterbury is where the serious writing began amidst the surroundings of a fairy tale city. Ruth Hall, your beautiful home in the Yogaville community nurtured my spirit and provided additional inspiration at a time I needed it most. Synchronicity Sanctuary, the place where it all began and where I was able to complete this book which became a process of deep healing and transformation.

Writing this book has been like running a marathon and every one of my friends and family members played a role to keep me moving forward, step by step, until it finally reached its beautiful conclusion. Most of all, I am so grateful for my sons Aaron and Adam—your presence in my life fuelled my motivation to keep going and not even consider giving up.